Contents

1
Golf's Holy Grail

Nathan's loud honking voice in the next room was really annoying. I was trying to get some work done and just couldn't tune him out. I could picture the scene; after all, it was the same every morning. He'd be there in the office reception holding forth, to anyone who'd listen, on any topic that floated into his brain. Ignorance never held Nathan back. He'd give his opinion on anything with the confidence of an expert. All of a sudden, in the midst of this stream of rubbish, something he said jumped out: "I could teach anybody to play golf to single figures in a summer."

Walking through, I found Nathan sitting on a desk clutching a steaming mug of tea. His idle boast had caught my attention. It seemed an unimaginable dream to have a golf handicap under ten. How could it be possible to achieve that in a single summer?

Nathan's simplistic view was that you don't have to play that well to be a single figure player. "You can still bogey every other hole," he said. On this topic Nathan had some credibility. He was a scratch player himself, a PGA pro, and had taught golf for several years.

It was a casual conversation, two minutes at most. Walking off, I could hear Nathan's booming voice already going on about something else. This brief exchange had been one of hundreds that happen in any normal day. Most are lost to the wind, but for some reason Nathan's comment took hold on my mind.

I went back to the States that winter, and phoned Nathan a couple of times to see if he really meant what he'd said.

Nathan's style on the phone was always short, almost to the point of rudeness. He'd just repeat his original comment in a tone of voice that sounded very like, "I don't really care if you believe me or not."

I had first taken up golf twenty years ago at the age of twenty-two. I had been very keen. I remember such huge excitement the first day I broke a hundred. My scores had come down to the low nineties that first year. The pinnacle of my previous golfing achievement had been breaking ninety twice. I think my best ever score had been eighty-eight.

For the past ten years I had basically quit the game. At best I played once a year, but I doubt I played even that much. I never made a decision to quit. Life had just been busy, with moving, travelling, birth of a business, marriage, and the birth of a child. A busy life had eclipsed golf. Those few times I played, my game had been a disaster, scores so high I dared not count. Sometimes there'd be a good shot, a distant echo of my vanished game.

For years I had a vague life goal of "one day" spending a summer to get my game together. Timing of that "one day" was in some imagined sunlit future – when I had time on my hands, I'd sold my business, was rich, my son had grown.

I dwelled on the tantalising concept: single figures in a summer. There was an odd feeling that the planets were lining up. This summer I would be in Ireland for two months and would have time to work on my golf. Nathan could be there to help, as August was going to be a quiet month for him.

Goals are cozy and comfortable when permanently in the future. There is an odd lurch when confronted with the possibility of taking a dream and making it real.

After much hesitation, I took the mental plunge: setting out on a quest for golf's holy grail – the single figure handicap. Making this decision, I had a feeling I remembered from years back as a kid at the swimming pool. Climbing the high diving board, standing on the end, I found that the longer one stands out there, the further the drop appears. Finally jumping, there's no going back.

The stage was set. I had exactly sixty days in Ireland to work on my golf with the goal of getting to a single figure handicap. Nathan would be with me the first three weeks.

I could never have imagined the adventures that this quest would bring. Of course I had no idea if I would succeed. Would I really end up playing golf to single figures?

The thing I could never have known was the wider, deeper, intriguing discovery that this quest would reveal.

2
The Assessment Round

*E*ight months after Nathan's "single figures in a summer" comment first caught my attention, I was standing on the first tee of an Irish golf course.

The plan today was to play nine holes. Nathan would walk around with me and at the end give an assessment of my game as it currently stood. I wondered what the verdict would be. I feared that when he saw how really bad my golf was, he would declare the situation hopeless and call the whole thing off. By the end of the afternoon I'd know the truth.

I don't think I'd actually kept score in a round of golf for years. Usually after three or four holes the numbers were so bad I gave up counting. I dreaded what this first score might be. How high can the number go?

I was nervous. Nathan wasn't helping. He usually looked a right mess but today had turned up very much dressed for the part, with neatly pressed logoed golf apparel head to toe. I felt scruffy beside him. Then there was this little blue notebook he'd produced. I came to dread that blue book as the day went on. As we waited for our slot on the tee, Nathan wrote furiously in this tiny book. I wondered what on earth he was writing. As I sidled round to look over his shoulder, he turned away, hiding the secret of what this book was about.

Nathan is best described as a bit of a character. I had worked with him for about five years. Nathan's office was so disgusting – countless mouldy coffee cups, cigarette butts everywhere, greasy fast food wrappers strewn across the floor, dank clothes and old socks draped the furniture –the office cleaner had quit. In fact, it was so disgusting it made me feel like quitting and I owned the company.

I have never seen anyone smoke a cigarette as fast as Nathan. Out on the course, he has this special way of casually flicking the cigarette butt away with thumb and forefinger, so it flies way out to the side as he walks fast, head down. He had spent seven years teaching golf fulltime and claimed he once coached a one-armed man to a seven handicap. Later he spent five years travelling the world caddying for the world's leading female golfers. He'd earned a pile of money doing this and invested it in drink and gambling. His language is appalling and he's very stroppy.

I had opened my golf bag the day before and found inside it a lost world. That bag hadn't been opened for six years.

My few impromptu games in recent years had been with rental clubs. I'd come to hate my own clubs, developing the mental fiction that I played better with rentals. I found a large stunt kite in the bag with the clubs. I have no idea why it was there. I found my eight iron missing. Years ago I'd left it beside a green at a London club. I'd called the pro to re-establish its whereabouts, but I was so uninterested in the game I never bothered to fetch it. Also in the bag was a tiny child's club bought for a young lady who is now almost as tall as me. A host of old score cards in one pocket brought back memories of rounds played long ago. I took a five iron outside for a couple of practice swings. My two-year-old son found this hilarious and aped my swing. His swing looked good. They say the swing should be a natural motion and comes easily to children.

At the first tee our behaviour was observed by a line of people sitting on the long wooden bench. It was a wonderful, sunny Sunday afternoon. The course was full. Everyone seems to play golf in Ireland, definitely not just the wealthy. A real mix of characters waited to play that 2,700-yard nine hole course beside the Irish sea with a ragtag mixture of golf clubs stuffed into old worn bags. No lines of gleaming golf cars or fancy equipment here! It was great to see them all waiting to play. Golf is definitely a healthy game around these parts. Sitting on the bench waiting their turn, they gradually moved up as each group went off. They watched us and I could see they thought us an odd couple. Two people, one set of clubs? What's with that writing in the little book?

"The View Out to Sea"

Has he brought his private teacher to the course? Who's he think he is?

As I moved up that long wooden bench, my turn on the first tee loomed closer. I felt this watching crowd wondering if I was some sort of good player bringing a teacher to the course. Having not hit a golf ball for over a year, I fully expected to scuff the ball ten yards to the ladies' tee. I wished I could just stay there on the bench and enjoy the beautiful view up the estuary and far out to sea – not have to play golf at all.

But the time had come. Up on the tee, the ball looked so tiny down there. Certain I'd whiff it, a 140 yard par three. Backswing, no going back now. Amazing. I hit it and a great shot too, right up there on the green. I walked off quickly, mightily relieved that the first tee and more particularly the line of watchers on the bench, were behind me. I babbled to Nathan that I didn't usually hit the ball like that. Nathan said nothing. On the green, I sank a ten foot putt for a birdie. More babbling that I didn't usually play like that. Nathan said nothing.

At the second tee, a beautiful three iron long and straight down the middle. I'd given up using woods years ago as my game fell apart. More comments from me that this wasn't my usual game. More silence from Nathan. With my fairway shot on the second my real game reasserted itself as I scuffed the ball twenty feet sideways into dense trees. It would be seven more rounds before I hit another green and twenty rounds before I got another birdie. The honeymoon was over.

The rest of that first nine hole assessment round became the usual degrading battle: my tee shots scudding along the ground, not even reaching the ladies' tees; playing my way down the right hand of each fairway from one clump of trees to another; multiple chips and putts; and repeatedly missing two foot putts. My mind started to count off how many more holes I had to endure. Five more to go. Three more to go. I took ten shots on the eighth. My thoughts increasingly rested on what I'd have to drink when I finally finished. Should it be a pint of Guinness or something stronger?

As we trudged up the hill to complete the ninth, the Irish rain closed in, soaking me. I supposed if I was going to spend the next two months working on my golf game in the green hills of Ireland I had better come to terms with getting wet. Strangely, in all the golf I played over the next couple of months, I only got wet once more.

Throughout the assessment round Nathan had written copious notes in that small blue book. His note-taking really annoyed me. Every time I did anything, he'd write in that book. Even when I didn't do anything he'd write in that book. I was intensely curious as to what all his notes where about. I finally managed to peer over his shoulder only to find that his handwriting was so tiny and such a mess, that I couldn't read a word. I actually wondered if even he could read this mess.

In the car driving the couple of miles into Kinsale for the warmth of an Irish pub, I finally asked Nathan for his verdict. I was very much concerned that he would say there was really no hope at all for my golf game and it would be better to call it a day right now. He said there was good news and bad news, but let's get a drink in front of us before we talked.

Finally, we were sitting in a nice cozy Kinsale pub on long stools up at the bar. A large fire roared behind us in the grate. A tank full of live lobsters gazed across at us. Clouds of cigarette smoke engulfed us. It was to be another six months before Irish law, very controversially, banned smoking in pubs. I felt thoroughly glad to be off the course, warm and dry and with a drink before me. I'd opted for the middle ground: a half of Guinness and a shot of Paddies, the local Irish whiskey. Out came Nathan's little blue book and on with the verdict.

Nathan asked if I wanted to start with the good news or the bad. I definitely wanted to start with the good stuff. It was this: two things were working. My swing tempo was excellent and I had a great eye for the ball. The bad news seemed endless. My grip had a weak left hand, right was too strong, poor overlap and I was holding the club in the palms like a baseball bat rather than in the fingers. I was gripping too hard. My stance was wide, leading to poor hip action, causing lateral movement rather than rotation. Leg action was bad. My ball position needed regulating. My aim was to the right. Elbows were closed. Balance good at address, lost with the swing. My take-away was in-to-out, primarily due to poor set up. Shoulders not rotating correctly. Nathan's final point was that I had a very negative attitude out on the course.

With all that going wrong, why wouldn't I have a negative attitude? I didn't really understand a word of what Nathan had just said; he may as well have been speaking a foreign language. I just didn't understand the lingo of golf tuition. It all sounded so terrible that the only conclusion must be that I should give up delusions of becoming a good golfer.

During my musings Nathan had started an animated discussion with his other neighbour at the bar. While I didn't understand a bean of what Nathan had said, this neighbour did. Soon they were up on their feet doing practice swings and threatening to send people's pints a-flying. Next the guy was asking if Nathan would give him some lessons.

Nathan's new friend was American, previously a stockbroker, but the dot com bust had assisted him in his new dream of living in Ireland. He was trying to get a visa to work in the country. It is kind of funny that after 150 years of the Irish, by hook or by crook, trying to get to America, the Celtic Tiger economy of the past decade has led to increasing numbers of Americans trying to get back to Ireland – a reverse Diaspora. For the first time since the potato famine in the 1840s, the Irish population is rising. We left the pub and I drove Nathan back to his cottage by the water. I felt deflated, with a complete sense of hopelessness about getting my game together. Nathan was ebulliently confident. He said without any doubt I could dramatically improve my game. He was very definite that I could get to a 15 handicap. He said, I could get to single figures if I put the work in, but I'd have to learn to chip and putt like a god. Nathan wanted to meet at the practice ground next day at 10 a.m. to hit balls.

Dropping Nathan off, wending my way back through the winding Irish rural roads, I pondered if I believed Nathan. Could I really become a good golfer? I wanted to believe, but in my heart I really didn't. Those negative thoughts again.

How Am I Doing? Day 1

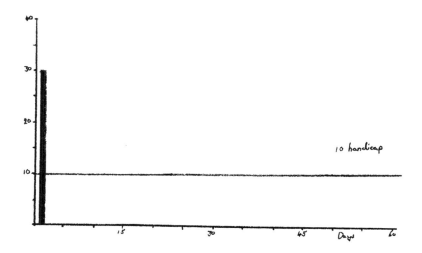

Looking at the score that first day of my assessment round, I saw that I'd shot fifty for a par thirty-five nine-hole. For the nine-hole round this suggests something in the region of a thirty handicap over a very easy 2,700 yard nine-hole with a standard scratch of sixty-six. As the graph starkly shows, I had a very long way to go to a ten handicap in sixty days.

3
The Grip

*T*en a.m. the next morning found us on the practice ground
at an eighteen-hole course ten miles inland, set amidst rolling hills and ancient trees beside a salmon river: Ireland at
its most luxuriant green.

The course was built within the remnants of an Irish
lord's massive estate. His legacy was mile upon mile of
high stone walls dissecting the land. The large golf practice field is bordered by these ten foot walls. One imagines
the countless years of manual labour needed to build these
walls hundreds of years ago; donkey and carts would have
hauled the rocks, each large stone lifted up by hand.

Years ago I'd driven the complete length of the west coast
of Ireland. Hour after hour we passed land that was divided into tiny fields by a dense latticework of stone walls.
One wonders at the centuries of human capital that must
have gone into their construction.

Back at the golf course these were no peasant walls of random stone marking tiny fields. These were the walls of a lord: high, straight, dressed stone. The oddest thing is that the purpose of the lord's walls is now lost. Why is that wall beside the practice area? What did it keep out? What did it keep in? Why was it built so high?

Nathan said, "Just bring the seven." So my only equipment was the Ping seven iron, a bag of ninety range balls and a coffee. In Ireland one doesn't find the super-size take-away coffee cups common in the States. The coffee tasted great but the cup was no bigger than the paper cup a dentist offers to rinse your mouth when the drill stops.

Now Nathan is all business about changing my grip. I plead with him about whether this is really necessary. At the last golf lesson I had, over ten years before, the pro had changed my grip. The experience was so terrible that I think it strongly contributed to my quitting the game. A grip change seems the most painful change to make. Nathan is very clear that there is no way I'm going to get better holding the club like I do. Fair enough. While I don't want to change the grip, my current one feels bad. The two hands seem to be fighting each other, leaving my arms tense.

It takes Nathan just a few minutes to show me the grip he wants: all this about holding the club in the fingers of the right hand, V's of the thumb and first finger pointing at the right shoulder. That sort of thing. Much of this I've heard before but remembered wrong. Nathan makes it very clear and simple. This is my first glimpse that for all his rough edges, here is a damn good teacher.

Nathan has me methodically apply the grip, finger by finger, each time, then hit the ball. To my amazement the new grip doesn't feel too bad. It feels more natural. With surprisingly little effort the ball seems to be going a long way. Nathan explains that the wrists can now release, giving greater club head speed. Cheerfully, he tells me that within a week the new grip will feel like the most natural thing in the world and that I won't wish to hold the club any other way. Keep with the new grip however strange it may feel at first. Nathan is very clear that under no circumstances am I to go back to the old grip, ever! I know Nathan's right, but it's so easy, finger by finger, to slip back into the old and more familiar ways.

I spend about half an hour hitting balls with the new grip. Nathan smokes cigarettes and the cows in the next field stare over the wall. I break every few swings for a sip from my dentist's cup of coffee. Nathan finally gives permission for reprieve.

We head out to the practice area to pick up the widely scattered balls. Nathan skirts the edge of the spread of balls, happily hitting the wider stragglers into the centre with casual one-handed chips, the inevitable cigarette in his other hand. I collect the balls with a picker. It's been twenty years since I last picked balls from a practice field like this. Returning to this simple chore brings back wonderful memories of my first few months of golf, friends and places long past. I've always enjoyed picking up the balls.

Mastering the golf swing was a challenge, but picking up balls I could do. I remember becoming obsessed with searching the rough edges of the practice ground for lost balls, trying to increase my ball stock every time I went out.

I was surprised that Nathan felt my set of Pings were the right clubs for me. I'd always heard that most people play with the wrong clubs. I'd bought these Pings second-hand years ago. I fully expected Nathan to have me down in the shop buying new clubs very quickly. I had also heard that many people don't need new clubs, they just need to re-grip the clubs they have. My clubs were fine, but the grips were not. Nathan showed me how my grips were worn to the point of slickness. This had me clutching the club too hard to avoid the feeling that the club might slip.

Rather than shelling out for new clubs, we were down in the golf shop buying new grips. Nathan didn't want to pay the extra two euros per club to have the grips fitted. He was happy to fit them himself that evening. We dropped into a hardware store in town for double-back tape, a sharp knife and white spirit.

I love Irish hardware stores. I have happy childhood memories of summers with my grandmother, visiting this very store. She would buy an assortment of unlikely items: blocks of peat that burned with a wonderful smell in her fireplace; aluminium pails with lids, with which we were sent up the hill to get milk from the creamery; sacks of seed potatoes; mantles for hurricane lamps; rolls of barbed wire to keep the cows from her vegetable garden.

Most extraordinary there was a garden tool she called "the slasher," a fearsome-looking curved blade set upon a long stick. I remember my tiny grandmother wielding that slasher, her white hair flowing in the wind as she hacked back the voracious fuchsia bushes that threatened, like Triffids, to envelop her house.

The hardware store is narrow, but endlessly long. As a child wandering into the depths of this store while my grand-mother negotiated her strange purchases, I got the distinct feeling of going back in history. Deeper in the store, it got darker, dustier and filled with ever more unlikely items from the past that had lain unsold for decades.

Finally back at the house I was glad the golf was over. Na-than wanted to meet again next day to work on the leg buckle. I was curious to find out what that was.

At this stage I definitely wasn't enjoying going out to play golf. I would far rather have sat on the old stone steps in front of the house, read a book and gaze out on the deep blue Irish sea.

We had been lent a wonderful old Georgian house for the summer. It was a house with layers of history. The cen-tral part was a beautifully proportioned Georgian hunting lodge. The Victorians had tagged on two winged exten-sions. More recent additions were a conservatory and tennis court. A labyrinth of out-houses in increasing layers of decay stretched out back. The oldest part was an old bell tower, the upper storey now the home of bats that swooped out into the evening dusk. The massive cracked walls of the tower were home to a voracious hive of bees.

I was determined to be a good student and surprise Nathan the next morning by being familiar with the new grip. After dinner I took a glass of wine and a golf club out to practice the grip on the front lawn. I heard years ago that when you take up golf the most important thing is to get completely comfortable with the correct grip. One could sit watching television, repeatedly putting the grip on the club over and over again. Doing this, the correct grip becomes second nature. I'd decided to spend an hour mindlessly repeating over and over again the act of putting the new grip on the club, then taking a practice swing.

According to Nathan, it is crucial to develop a consistent routine when addressing the ball. Whether casually practising, or hitting the most important shot of your life, one should go through exactly the same routine every single time. So out there on the front lawn, with a beautiful view of the sea down the valley, my glass of wine on the stone steps, I worked on the grip. Repeatedly I picked up the club and methodically, finger by finger, assembled my new grip, took my stance and made a swing.

I set myself the task of going through this routine a hundred times. Initially this seemed pointless and boring. Very soon, I enjoyed a great sense of peace. Every few swings I stopped for a sip of wine. I felt profoundly happy. This is my first memory of actually enjoying spending time on my golf since taking up this sixty-day quest.

It was a beautiful evening. Dusk was drawing in and faint sounds drifted up the valley: a dog barking, the hum of distant farm machinery. Flocks of crows circled overhead, getting ready to roost for the night in the ancient trees that surrounded this house.

The bird life in these parts of Ireland is amazing. I remember one time taking some visiting friends of mine who were interested in birds and showing them one hundred different species of bird in a single day. For people into birds, that's a big deal.

Each day, on the point in front of my father's house, there's a daily rhythm of the birds. As the beach to the west is covered by the tide, huge flights of birds fly around to the eastern beach to get another couple of hours feeding before that beach too is covered. For about an hour formation after formation of birds pass the point. As a child I used to imagine them to be wartime formations of bombers or fighter planes: the V-shaped formations of curlew passing high overhead; formations of black and white oyster catchers moving fast just a few feet above the sea; pairs of cormorants like modern-day stealth bombers; and lapwings passing so close, the whirr of six thousand wings fills your ears.

Every day an extraordinary, joyful aerial display. Tens of thousands of birds. Repeated as the tides reverse and the birds return as the beaches are uncovered.

When I was young my father pointed out that this same wondrous display of birds has been going on every day exactly the same for tens of thousands of years.

At night, walking back from the local pub, you'd hear these birds out there on the tidal flats feeding. In the stillness of the night the birds had their own symphony going on, a huge sound. One group would start off out in the darkness, then from a different area other birds with different calls, the music would move and swell as though directed by an unseen conductor. Often I would stop under the dense canopy of stars enthralled by the sound.

4
The Leg Buckle

*D*éjà vu: it's ten a.m. and here I am, on the same practice ground, with a seven iron and another dentist's cup of coffee. The same cows look over the wall. The lord's walls still stretch long and straight. Today Nathan is all excitement about working on the leg buckle. He has the Pings he regripped the evening before. I can't believe the improvement. The new grips really feel sticky. They exude a reassurance that they won't slide from my hands. I can certainly see now why Nathan called the old ones "slick."

I take a few practice swings to warm up. Nathan declares, "You've taken the grip well." His understated praise means a great deal to me. My practice in the gloaming of the previous day has paid off.

Nathan launches into his explanation of the leg buckle. He shows that at the top of the backswing, the body is like a wound spring. The part of the body that wants to unwind first is the shoulders. However, it's really the hips, driven by the legs, that should start the unwind. Nathan does two demonstration swings. In the first, the correct one, the hips start the unwind. The second is the wrong way, the shoulders starting the unwind. From the range we can look out over the course and watch several groups of players. Nathan points out that the higher handicap players let their shoulders come through first, while the good players have strong leg action that brings the hips through first. It's getting the power of the legs into the swing that gives the effortless distance.

The point has been well made by Nathan. I understand what it's supposed to look like, what it's not supposed to look like and how to make it happen. Nathan says the swing thought, at the top of the backswing, starting the forward swing, is "locking the leg." He does a slow-motion swing, freezing at impact, showing how his left leg is locked solid at the knee as the ball is struck. It surprises me that the left leg would or could be locked solid upon impact. This is so different from my mental image of how the golf swing works. It seems physically impossible! Fair enough, there's Nathan doing it, so it must be possible.

I set up to hit balls, the swing mantra "lock the leg, lock the leg, lock the leg," singing in my head. Wow, what a disaster. Can't hit the ball. Some complete whiffs, the rest bouncing along the ground a few yards. Nathan, fully relaxed, says, "Hit away. It'll come, it'll come."

Changing the actual swing motion, to me, is the hardest thing. I was much heartened the previous day when Nathan said that ninety percent of the golf swing is the setup. He said the six elements of the set up were: alignment, grip, feet position, ball position, body alignment and stance. All of this I felt I could do. It was just a matter of rote learning and practice, practice, practice. I'd already made great progress on the grip. But the swing motion's a different thing. All of it happens so damned quick. A pro's swing can be one point seven seconds from the start of the take-back to the very end of the follow-through. These swings look so slow, it's amazing the ball goes so far. Out of this apparently graceful slowness comes huge club head speed just at the point of impact. The amateur's swing is more like one second: short, snatchy, too fast. Honestly, what can you do to change something that's all over within a second?

I suppose it's obvious that people come with different levels of athletic ability. Along the continuum of gifted athlete to complete klutz, I'm pretty far out there on the klutz end of things. What first drew me to golf was the fact that the ball is stationary when you hit it, seemingly cutting the problem in half compared to other sports, where the ball is moving around before you have to catch it or hit it.

School sport had been degrading for me. I was the one left standing when the two teams were picked. Sport at my English school was all about rugby in the winter and cricket in the summer. With virtually no ability to throw or catch, I wasn't a lot of use to either. Cricket had me consigned to the furthest reach of the outfield and things seldom happen that far out. I've always had great sympathy

for Pluto, almost 4,000 million miles from the Sun, where
one Pluto year is 248 Earth years. That's pretty much what
it feels like to be way out in deep field on a cricket pitch. I
remember lying on my back watching the vapour trail of a
plane make its lazy way across the blue of an English summer sky, when distant shouts from the white-clad figures
around the wicket, alerting me of things coming my way.
I would be up just in time to see the small red leather ball
bounce over the boundary line. Failed again.

In the experiment of seeing if it was possible to radically
improve one's golf game in sixty days, I was a great guinea
pig. With my klutsy sporting ability, if I could do it, anybody could.

Back to reality at the practice ground, I've been hitting
away and Nathan has smoked a whole pile of cigarettes.
Laid out before us is a rather depressing pattern of range
balls scattered in a wide arc before us. Few balls have gone
further than thirty yards. I'm suffering from an extreme
urge to take a break, I suggest to Nathan that we go for
coffee in the clubhouse, or breakfast. I feel sure the clubhouse will have a wonderful Irish breakfast: eggs, bacon,
black pudding, white pudding, fried tomatoes, fried mush-
rooms, fried bread. The works. A cardiologist's nightmare. Nathan's having nothing to do with taking a break,
just mutters, "It'll come, it'll come," puffing his cigarette,
staring at the cows as the cows stare back at him.
Eventually, by bashing away with the swing thought, "lock
the leg, lock the leg," balls start to get airborne. Improve-

ment, but still a shadow of how I'd started the morning. Prior to trying to fix this damn leg buckle I'd been hitting the seven 150 yards and sort of straight. Now, I am pleased to get the ball off the ground and fifty yards out. This is terrible. I am mightily relieved when Nathan runs out of smokes, calling it a day.

Back at the Georgian house that evening, I wondered if I could repeat the success of the day before with the grip. Out on the front lawn again, looking down over the sea, seven iron and glass of wine, I set myself to practice one hundred swings, trying the leg lock thing.

I didn't get any of the sense of peace I'd experienced the previous evening. Getting this change of leg action to feel right was frustrating and in a strange way disturbing. Also my body hurt. I had been good and fit starting into this golf quest just three days ago, but now, my whole body was sore. Being fit for one sport, then switching to another, always gets the muscles aching. Fit as you like, but those first few days of skiing really get to you. Same for any sport the body's not used to. Having not swung a golf club for years, it wasn't just aching muscles; even my bones seemed to hurt.

To me it seemed that one of the biggest risks in this sixty day push to get my game together would be picking up an injury. A bad back seemed a pretty good candidate to bring things to a halt.

Advil is a wonderful thing at times like this. In the lock-er rooms of crusty posh clubs, I've seen bottles of Advil larger than a gallon carton of ice cream. All those old guys gulping them down. Once I met the man who brought Advil to America. He thought Advil was great. He would; he made a ton of money from it. He told me it was a great idea to take Advil ahead of the exercise. I certainly had my bottle of Advil back in the cupboard.

Stretching, too, is a wonderful thing at times like this. Liv-ing in San Francisco, it seemed everyone had green yoga mats under their arms. I got into yoga, too. After years of running and other abuses of the body I had a bad back, bad hip and bad shoulder. Yoga, like magic, fixed all these prob-lems. Also, yoga is the toughest workout I've ever done. A strange thing: one never moves off the mat, one never moves fast, but twenty minutes into a yoga routine you're sweating more than anything I've ever experienced doing, including half-marathons, triathlons and circuit training.

It was through yoga that I came to the idea of doing a sixty day program to improve my golf. Bikram, a famous yogi, had come to San Francisco to give a lecture. Out of curios-ity, I'd gone along. There must have been three thousand people there. Bikram had a special talent for making you feel irritated, or even darn right angry with him. During his talk, he jabbed his finger at the audience and angrily shouted, "you do Bikram yoga for thirty days and you will see the difference!" The odd thing was, after all his provocation, rather than having the rational reaction of walking out of his lecture and going for a nice cold beer, I thought to myself, damn you, I'll do that.

Bikram yoga is the marine boot camp of yoga. In a 106° Fahrenheit room, it is an incredibly tough ninety-minute workout, the hardest physical thing I've ever done. I really hated those classes at the start. Thirty days later, I felt an amazing difference. I ended up doing sixty days. I couldn't believe the change it made physically, mentally and in almost every aspect of my life. I wondered if bringing the same sixty day intensity to golf could work similar miracles for my game.

Advil, yoga and wine. A trinity, but not a holy one. Hopefully this would keep my body together for sixty days of golf.

5

Early Morning Golf for the First Time

The plan was to play nine holes at six o'clock every morning. The early morning idea was partly to get a golf course unencumbered by other golfers so we could practice. I was also keen to be out there on my own, as I was embarrassed by my game.

Setting the alarm for 5:15 a.m. would give me time to get out of the house, drive to Kinsale and get my clubs and gear ready to tee off by six. The night's sleep ahead of that first early start was fitful. I woke every half hour to see what time it was, worrying about oversleeping and leaving Nathan standing on the early morning tee wondering where I was. It certainly didn't help that I'd been at the pub too late drinking too many pints.

The local pub was called the Pink. Walking in there is always an adventure. A pack of kids out front frolicked across the expanse of lawn and the breathtaking view out to sea. An ancient man, snaggle-toothed and buckle-legged, made tottering progress toward the bar. I joke to him as I pass, pointing to the wooded headland a half mile across the water, "Would that be America?" The lightning fast comeback as a skinny arm pointed at the little fishing village: "And that would be Manhattan." We both laughed.

Pushing the door open, a tight pack of people between me and the bar, the broad back of the Piano Player dwarfing the old upright against the wall, his huge hands assaulting the keys, his music filling the room, the landlord's black dog, the only lab I've ever known to growl at everyone.

Pushing through the crowd trying to get to the bar. The laughter of two buxom young waitresses making lewd jokes about the dessert trolley, the Englishman complaining about the prices, the landlord's two small children, always in party dresses, serving drinks and clearing tables, the black-haired man with scary tattoos glaring at his pint, the funeral party full of jolly smiles and drink.

Pushing through, pushing through. The communion party, the flutter of white dresses, small sandwiches and cakes, the loud-talking German; a glimpse of the landlord's wife out back, dressed to the nines, but never coming front-of-house; the dark crowd in the TV room, the small fuzzy screen hanging from the ceiling always on sport.

Pushing through, pushing through. A lady by the piano breaks out in song, nervous smiles of two American tourists in neatly pressed golf shirts. The tall lobster fisherman looks clear over the crowd. The stalk-like figure of the parish priest by the bar, propped up by his walking stick and a tumbler of whiskey.

Pushing through, pushing through. Raucous singing of a team, parading an enormous silver trophy wanting everyone to drink from the scary dark liquid sloshing within. Children run everywhere, weaving between the legs of the crowd. The drunk at the bar who's had too much, offered a drink "I shouldn't but I will."

Pushing through, pushing through.

The smart older couple out for a meal look completely shocked when offered a drink while standing in the midst of a pub "Well, I think I'll have a small sherry." There's the pig farmer, the big farmer, the small farmer. The eager smile of the man from up and the creamery, but you can never understand a word he says. Big Tom at the bar. Round red faces of the lads perched in a circle on tall stools, not speaking, but smiling at their pints. The booming voice of the Jolly Banker as he organizes a round of drinks.

Pushing through, finally reaching the bar. A bar made from the broken half of an old wooden clinker-built boat. Some say the landlord found it wrecked on the rocks out at the Old Head, others say he ran his own boat up on the rocks. You never can get a straight story out of the landlord.

A tiny baby, wrapped in a blue blanket, fast asleep on the bar. The broad jolly face of the barman and there beside him Mad Bill the landlord thrusts his face into yours, intense eyes and huge black eyebrows. "So what will it be?"

Mad Bill has owned the Pink as long as any of us can remember. Just about every local I know, at some stage has been "banned for life" from the Pink by Bill. The odd thing about being banned for life is you usually have no idea what you've done wrong. If banned, the thing to do, is to do nothing, say nothing and certainly don't remonstrate with Bill. Just leave. Come back a few days later and nothing more will be said.

Sometimes when you go back, by way of apology Bill will slide a free pint across the bar to you with his finger. Never say a word or look you in the eye. Sometimes when you go back Bill will just throw you out again.

You'd think the locals would go somewhere else, but the problem is it's a long way to the next pub and it's great fun in the Pink.

One evening I'd been talking with Bill at the bar when two policemen, or Gardai as they're called in Ireland, came in. I leaned my head into Bill's and whispered, "I think they've come to take you away." He muttered back, "It'll take more of 'em than that to get me out of here." We looked at each other and laughed heartily. I know we both shared the same mental image of several vanloads of Gardai battling Bill to drag him from his domain.

Mad Bill had been the face behind the bar at the Pink all our lives but there was talk this year that he was thinking of selling the place.

A big night at the Pink would see the place packed. The piano player could play anything if you bought him a pint of Guinness. As the evening got late there'd be pints lined right across the top of that old piano, wrong notes flying from his fingers, the music getting louder and faster, the ancient instrument shaking to the tune being hammered out, the throng of people singing, dancing if they could find the space. There are pub closing times in Ireland, a certain time when, by law, the place should shut and people go home. At the Pink this law was interpreted to mean that the door would shut and the curtains shut, but the bar stayed open. If you were in, you could stay in til you felt like going home. It was sometimes dawn before people felt like going home.

Despite the late night at the Pink, I woke next morning ahead of the alarm and was up and out the door in a matter of minutes. My head was swimming with tiredness. I'm no early morning person. Not often seeing this end of the day, I was amazed by the beauty of the landscape. The sea was mirror–calm and mist flowed down the valleys. The early morning light rendered everything sharper, clearer, almost a Van Gogh yellow. Not a soul was about.
At the course, Nathan is already standing on the tee with his inevitable cigarette. We have the place to ourselves; not even the greens staff are there. It's great to tee off without

the watchers on the bench. Our only companion is a large hare observing from the ladies' tee and it lollops away as we walk past. Down in the bay is a half sunk boat that hadn't been there before.

My golf is terrible, much worse than the first round. A score of fifty for the first nine-hole round has risen to fifty-two in round two. This doesn't upset me. I expected to get worse before I got better. I know enough that when one starts rebuilding the swing fundamentals one has to weather some bad golf. Along the holes down by the water, each fairway is covered by a sea of rabbits – hundreds of them. You can see where they were digging great holes into the bunker walls and earth banks, a nightmare for the greens staff.

My grip feels great but it doesn't seem to me that much progress has been made on the leg action. Nathan claims my legs are better. My putting is awful; I four-putt several greens.

During the last few holes a good strong cup of Irish tea and breakfast are very much on my mind. Driving back to the house at around eight a.m., I feel mighty worthy. The score wasn't great but I'd got the early morning ball rolling.

The return drive took me past one of the great beaches of this coast, a wide expanse of golden sand. The tidal range in these parts is large, low tide revealing endless flats of sand, high tide bringing the water to lap the very edge of the road.

There is a monthly rhythm to the tides. Once each month, sun and moon line up, resulting in a spring tide, with particularly high, then low, water. It's always fun, at these very low waters, to walk out over the sands and amidst rocks that are seldom uncovered. Sometimes, due to low pressure systems, wind, or some other mysterious magic of the planet, the spring tide brings weirdly low water. The tide goes out, then keeps going out, then goes out further than any local can remember. One walks out on areas nobody can ever recall being uncovered, stands on rocks never before seen, walk way out over stretches of sand usually deep, deep under water.

The oddest thing, at the turn of these unnaturally low tides, is that the tide seems to pulse. One would think it's a simple matter that the tide goes out, then comes in. But no: standing out there on the sand, where six hours from now the water will be twenty feet over your head, you watch the tide start to move in, then recede, then move in. Pulsing. You wonder if you are witnessing some primal heartbeat of the planet. When the spring tide really turns, it comes fast. In my memory people have drowned out on these sands caught by the tides. Many people.

Recent summers had seen big deposits of weed dumped along the high tide mark of the local beaches. This weed was causing great consternation in the area. The weed was not the normal healthy seaweed washed up on the shore after storms. It was a new, bright green, lettuce-like weed. It didn't seem a healthy thing but nobody could be sure.

Weed would seem a funny thing to fuss about, but as it lay on the beaches it started to rot. Mounds of this stuff blackened and stank, ruining those golden beaches. Among many of the people there was a strange reaction: denial. On the beach they would look out as though seeing golden sand and blue sea, rather than the rotting weed mounded before them.

The denial approach to the weed reminded me of our cat when I was a child. He was a big cat and a voracious birder. No bird was too big for him to take on: fat pigeons, magpies, large jackdaws – he'd take all comers. Afraid of nothing, this cat. One summer a large and very splendid peacock escaped from somewhere nearby and came to live in the garden for a few weeks. Rather than admit defeat when confronted by this huge bird, the cat would sit with complete indifference, gazing across the garden as the peacock strutted the lawn a few feet away. The cat never acknowledged the bird even existed.

As the summer wore on and the weed piled higher on the beaches, denial gave way to a search for truth and round after round of unlikely theories were unearthed, examined, discarded, to explain this awful weed.

6
It Rains Really Hard

Day six brings big rain, all day. Tipping it down. The Irish would say, "Ah, 'tis a soft day." To those not of the green hills, this is a day to stay inside. Nathan turns up very grumpy about the weather and installs himself in the kitchen, smoking, drinking tea and peering at the tiny screen of his mobile phone, occupying himself texting his mates.

The weather breaks and Nathan declares it's time for pitching practice. He tells me to find buckets, so I go looking in the outhouses. All these big old Irish houses are backed by the most wonderful outhouses. Originally for servants, stables, cowsheds, cheese making, carriages, hay storage and other activities of rural life, a village of industry behind every great house. Today they languish in various stages of decay, full of delicious junk. As a kid I loved exploring outhouses. My favorite were the most decayed, the most ruinous, the one at the end with no roof, just walls with vacant shapes of windows and doors long gone. Even better shadows of weed-covered walls allowing a child's imagination to conjure what might have been.

These outhouses are rich in discovery: several old cars in increasing states of decay, a rotting boat, horse tackle, remnants of cow stalls, agricultural tools, oil drums, a collection of small wooden school room furniture stacked to the ceiling and everywhere broken glass and old birds' nests. A small green door reveals a large room with a pool table. Thick layers of dust cover everything, evidence of the room sitting silent and undiscovered for many years. Colored balls on the table, a half-played game abandoned long ago.

Emerging on the front lawn, I hand Nathan a pile of old buckets. He starts striding about the soggy grass with random purpose like he's deciphering a pirate map. "Ten paces north from ye old tree, eight paces to the setting sun" – that sort of thing. Returning to a corner of the lawn, Nathan reveals his purpose. He explains that from this corner the buckets are laid out at different distances in different directions. Nathan demonstrates "the game," as he calls it: pitch three balls at one bucket, three at the next, so on and so on. The game gets one used to pitching to different distances on different lines. No big lesson on how to pitch. "Just do what's comfortable," he says. Nathan, with an effortless slow-motion swing, plops balls down by the different buckets. Frequent clangs from the buckets as he scores direct hits.

Random, rather than accurate, is a better word to describe my performance. Picking up the balls, I see that Nathan's are all in tight clusters around the buckets. My shots are so widely scattered it's hard to know which bucket I'd been aiming at. Rain stops play; we trudge back into the old house as the downpour returns.

No rest for the weary; time for carpet putting. The old house has a wonderfully long, wide corridor. A Georgian gallery is a better description, with proportions that make one feel like a prince every time one walks it. Lining both walls are generations of family portraits. The gallery oozes history. Just what's needed for putting practice? Nathan reckons, "That carpet's stimping about eight."

Emerging from the library with a pile of dusty books, Nathan sets two books down in the middle of the corridor, obviously meant to be the hole. Fifteen feet from the hole Nathan, with great care, creates two more book piles, just wide enough for the putter head to pass through. The concept: swing the putter through this gap. In order not to knock the books over, the putting stroke must be completely straight. Any in to out, or out to in and the books get knocked over. I step up to have a go – no ball, just some practice swings. Even with the greatest of care, I keep hitting the right of the outside book. Nathan triumphantly declares, "There you are: your putting stroke is out-to-in."

There are three kids playing in the house. It's the strangest thing. This is a big house, a very big house, but the only place the kids can think of playing is in the fifteen-foot space directly between myself and the books marking the

"The Old House"

hole. We move their first game up and around the corner. In no time they have a second game going right there in front of the hole. Every five minutes they're back. It's like shooing seagulls from a pile of fish. Between the thunderous Irish rain on the mould-green slate of the three-hundred-year-old roof and the kids playing directly where I'm aiming, I try to keep my head together enough to putt.

With more practice I'm now able to swing the putter through the books without knocking them over, but there's still no ball. When I putt with the ball, the books come tumbling down. It's amazing – I can do this perfectly fine without the ball, but put the ball in play and the swing changes! I'm to find in the next few weeks that this is a common problem. One's practice swing is often different from the swing one puts on the ball. So much of this game is in the mind, all in the mind.

With more practice, I'm able to swing through the books with the ball in play. The focus now is getting the ball in the hole – those other books, fifteen feet up the corridor. Some balls do go in, but these are few. My shots have an even spread from six inches left to six right. Extremely variable.

"Work on that, it'll get better," says Nathan, who then demonstrates the next "game." Nathan putts a ball clean, through the hole, leaving it twenty feet further up the corridor. He putts successive balls through the hole, each coming to rest two feet shorter than the previous one to leave a neat line of balls in two feet intervals. This exercise is to work on putting strength. It would take me many hours of practice in that long corridor, as the ancestors looked down, before I could come even close to what Nathan had done with such casual ease.

My third round of golf. Another early morning start at Kinsale. This early morning thing is already becoming easier. I'm in the car and driving down the lane just minutes after crawling out of bed. It's amazing how much of our lives we waste in transition between one thing and the next. Getting going in the morning, for me, is usually an hour and a half of reading the paper, breakfast, shower, etc. A sense of purpose concertinas all this into four or five minutes. The Duke of Wellington had a favorite saying: "Time to roll over, time to roll out." He was an early riser. Apparently he was up at two a.m. on the day he fought Waterloo, after averaging just three or four hours sleep each night for the week prior to the battle.

My new-found early morning efficiency has me on the course half an hour early. I use this time to follow Nathan's constant admonition: practice putting. My brother, who has stoically played eighteen holes every Saturday morning for the past twenty years – rain, wind, shine, or even snow – recently saw a marked drop in his scores by following the seemingly simple dictum of spending fifteen minutes putting before going out. These few minutes of putting before each round took more of his score than lessons and a new set of clubs.

It is gloriously peaceful on the putting green in the still silence of the morning. The early light imbues the view with added clarity. The sunken boat remains in the estuary. The large hare, again, sits by the first tee, as if to say "good morning." Eventually, the silence is broken by Nathan's car bouncing up the gravel track. I feel proud to be here before him and discovered actually doing some work.

That second early morning round is awful. Nothing seems to be working and I have a feeling of frantically flailing at the ball. On the third tee, I ask Nathan to show me how it should be done. Until this point, I haven't seen Nathan hit a single ball apart from a few casual one-armed chips. Using the three iron, Nathan beans a couple of perfect draws. The two balls now sit just a couple of feet apart, two hundred yards down the fairway. It is the casual ease and lack of any apparent physical effort that make the strongest impression. Handing the club back to me with a stretch of the back, Nathan says, "those are the first ones I've hit this year." I suppose once you've got it, you've got it.

I found it hugely helpful to see Nathan hit those two balls. It proved it could be done. There's a wonderful concept: Sheldrake's theory of morphic resonance. Sheldrake, a Cambridge and Harvard educated academic, conducted a slew of studies looking at things like how quickly people solve crossword puzzles or how quickly rats find their way through a maze. He found that if a crossword puzzle had already been solved in London, people given the same puzzle in New York, on average, could solve it faster. He found the same sort of thing with rats. If a rat had already found its way through a particular maze, rats confronted with the same maze, anywhere else in the world, would find their way through it quicker. Sheldrake's theory is: if something has already been done, it becomes easier for the next person. It doesn't matter where this next person is or that they know it's been done before. Sheldrake offers no explanation as to why this effect exists apart from some odd stuff about there being some resonance in the universe that connects everything. What is most entertaining about Sheldrake's theory is how much it annoys his fellow academics. They see it as one of their own turning against them; a top-notch scientist, using proper scientific method, has come up with a theory that is totally pixelated.

If all this Sheldrake stuff is true, Tiger Woods playing amazing golf should lift my game. Tiger probably raised the level on the tour but hasn't had any effect that I can measure at my humble level. But seriously, being around good players does help ones game. Certainly as I struggled that morning at Kinsale it was enormously encouraging to see Nathan hit those balls. In the same fashion, playing with good players, if it's not too intimidating, brings you up, showing you how to go at the course.

When I first took up golf, two decades ago, there was a video called "Cybervision." The video was sixty minutes of a pro hitting the ball over and over again, going through each club in the bag: driver, down through the irons and finally, the putter. It was hypnotic. It burned into the brain that wonderful pro tempo.

Attending a pro tournament, it can be quite surprising to see the tour pros hit in real life. TV gets us up close to the action, but does dumb down the spectacle. Standing right by a tour pro, the first shock is seeing how far they hit the ball. The second surprise is how slow they swing and how little apparent effort is made. Watching them on the practice range, they do these slow graceful swings. The ball goes up, then when ones eye expects it to come down, it seems to just keep going up, up and up. It's almost an optical illusion, those effortless swings creating such powerful shots. We amateurs all swing too quickly. Being around those pros, with their slow tempos, can help slow us down.

The third round at Kinsale was my worst yet. Nine holes on a short and easy course and I had a score of fifty-five. So far, every time I'd played my scores got worse: fifty, fifty-two, fifty-five. I was not discouraged because I knew at the start that when rebuilding the swing, you get worse before getting better.

We stopped for a cup of tea at the tiny clubhouse as we finished the round. The TV was on and the Icelandic singer Björk was singing a Marilyn Monroe song. The club manager, with the broadest of Scottish accents, recounted the story of a New Year's Eve party at the clubhouse some years earlier when thick snow fell across the course. The members had danced to Auld Lang Syne by the eighteenth green, as the snow fell and the New Year came in.

Later that day, I did some work pitching at the buckets on the front lawn. I'd put some good time in at those buckets and felt I'd made progress when my friend, the Hurley Player, breezed up all chipper about life in general. Hurling is a hugely popular field sport in Ireland. At first glance, it looks like field hockey; the ball, the field and the stick are roughly the same. The biggest difference is, the stick can be raised above the shoulder for taking big swings at the ball. Good players can send the ball from one end of the pitch to the other. It's like golf in the air. The Irish proudly call it the fastest field sport in the world. It probably is.

Hurling is exciting to watch but appears hugely violent. Heads regularly seem to get in the way of those wildly swinging sticks. A good game is deemed to be when the other team goes home sore. Fights break out regularly. There's a rule that you are not supposed to be on the field with an openly bleeding wound. One often sees the spectacle of a huge hurley player standing on the touch line remonstrating with a frightened and rather small, paramedic that blood is not really gushing out of his forehead and that he should be let back into the game. Later, asking this player, who happened to be a top lawyer in town, what on earth he was doing getting into that fight, you get the response, "I had a duty to protect my team mates."

Anyway, that's hurling and here was my friend the Hurley Player, who had been one of the leading hurlers in the area. Like all athletes, he couldn't resist trying to make a game out of my pitching practice and quickly had a money bet on who could get closest to the buckets. By this time, I had spent several hours practising at those damn buckets. With no practice at all, the Hurley Player began cheerfully dinging balls off the buckets and taking more of my money with every ding.

7
Hitting the Wood for the First Time in Years

Nathan and I meet up again in the evening on the practice ground at Bandon. These courses may be deserted in the morning, but are packed in the evening. People are turning up to start playing at eight p.m. Those Irish summer nights can be long and in midsummer it's still light at eleven. A weird gloaming can linger until eleven-thirty. Nathan wants to get me back using the woods. I'd dropped the woods from my bag years ago. I was just too erratic. Falling back to a long iron off the tee cost me length, but at least I was in the fairway. The woods retreat helped my score. They say the driver tells the truth. Any swing errors will be amplified. My driver problem was more psychological. I'd look down at that big driver head and this craze would fill my brain that I had to hit this really hard. Swinging hard produced terrible results.

Nathan sets me up with a Callaway three wood and has me hit a few. Having literally not put my hand on a wood

for years, the results are awful. Nathan then goes through
a process of tuning me down to almost nothing. He has me
hitting just with a flick of my wrists, not moving my arms,
legs or shoulders at all. Only my wrists moving. This wrist
flick sends the ball almost a hundred yards. It's amazing! Introducing a bit of volume control, I'm next allowed
to move the hands one foot back. Now the ball is going
over one hundred yards. Next the hands can go back to
shoulder level and the ball is now going down the field almost two hundred yards. What these exercises show, with
extraordinary elegance, is how little effort is needed with
a wood to make the ball go a very long way. Less is definitely more, so much more. As we finish and walk down
the hill, I am struck by the extraordinary beauty and stillness of this Irish summer evening.

That same evening the local lawyer, or solicitor as they
are called in these parts, got thrown out of the Pink. He
was sitting there having a nice quiet drink when Bill appeared and immediately banned him for wearing shorts
and bringing his dog. As he was ejected there was a look of
confusion on his face, everyone else in the place was wearing shorts on that warm evening and there was Bill's own
dog sitting up by the bar growling. We will never know
if this incident led directly to the lawyer, next summer,
opening a restaurant in the next village in direct competition with Bill.

We carry on the work at the range next morning. I hit for
half an hour before Nathan arrives and I continue practis-

ing the wrist flick thing. It seems magical, getting so much distance with so little effort. With Nathan, I hit another eighty balls. No great pressure, just hitting away with the three wood, trying to keep the swing slow and measured.

We retired to the clubhouse for a coffee. Mentally, at this early stage of my golf quest, I really needed to take these breaks. There had been a lot of golf in the past week, tiring on a body not used to golf. It was tiring on the brain, too. Nathan was saying he had to go back to London next week, to get his hip looked at. He had some dreadful degenerative hip thing that was going to lead to a hip replacement in his mid thirties – about now. I felt a great sense of unease that we had just really got started and now Nathan was leaving.

8
First Putting Lesson

My putting is in need of a huge dose of help. Three and four putting greens is common for me. I literally can't even get a two-foot putt in the hole. If I could crack two simple things, my game would be radically better. First, get the ball off the tee and into the fairway. Secondly, sink a two-foot putt.

In the early stage of getting a golf game together, it's a difficult thing to allocate time to putting practice. The big crisis is just getting the ball down the fairway without looking like a complete idiot. Putting seems a nicety when one can't get the ball off the tee, rather like spending time polishing the brass work when the ship is sinking. I had bigger things to worry about. The fact is that the crisis of getting the ball down the fairway solves itself remarkably quickly if one follows the right steps. However, later in the process, the score comes from the chips and putts. Looking back on this adventure of getting my game together I wish I'd started to put more time into chipping and putting far earlier in the process.

Nathan's big point is that my putting alignment is wrong. This is posh talk for bad aim. He searches about the putting green for a straight uphill putt. I would find this to be a good trick for my later putting practice: find a straight putt with absolutely no break. This allows one to work on the putting stroke without the added complication of the break. It's hard to find a completely straight putt on a golf green; the easiest to find are usually the uphill ones.

Now, satisfied he's found a straight putt, Nathan has me do a few four-foot putts; predictably, I miss the lot. I'm set up to do another when Nathan grabs the putter and holds it exactly where I had it. He tells me to let go of the club and walk around behind the putter face and see where I'd been aiming. I am astonished; the putter is clearly aimed eight inches right of the hole from four feet out. I was convinced I'd aimed that putter directly at the hole. My visual perception of aim, clearly, was completely off. It's no wonder that these short putts seldom went in. I wasn't aiming at the hole.

Laying two clubs down, Nathan creates tramlines along the four feet from ball –to hole. With these tramlines in place, there can be no mistake on the aim. The putter face has to be at right angles to the tramlines. With the tramlines every putt goes straight in the hole, time after time after time. It's a great feeling.

This tramline demonstration was hugely helpful. It showed that I'd been aiming my putts all wrong. Looking down at each putt, I'd feel this mental jar that I was aiming left even though the tramlines clearly showed my aim being correct. Nathan said if I worked away with the tramlines, I'd readjust my mental perception of aim.

The second big lesson of the tramlines was getting putts in. I had become so used to missing putts that I kind of expected to miss. It was a revolutionary feeling, sinking putt after putt. I kept hitting away at that four-foot putt, loving the sound of each ball dropping in the hole. I must have sent a couple of hundred balls down those tramlines and into the hole.

This reminded me of a conversation that I had with a wonderful and ancient Irish aunt of mine twenty years ago. She was a grand lady, had travelled all over the world, wore huge hats and had cocktails every afternoon. At the time she was in her late eighties and tragically had all but lost her sight to glaucoma. I was telling her I'd recently taken up golf. She revealed that she used to love golf. In fact, she had been a seven handicap but had quit the game when she started falling into the bunkers due to her failing eyes. Way back then I found putting frustrating. On telling my aunt, her reaction was, "It's easy, my dear! Just stand there and put a hundred short putts in. You'll get so used to them going in that all the putts start going in."

Nathan originally didn't want to mess around with my putting grip, but as he watches, he feels there is too much wrist in my putt. He has me pause and watch the other players practising on the putting green. There's a ladies' competition going off the first, so the putting green has a lot of players tuning their putting, ready for competition; some of the players are very good. Nathan points out how some keep their wrists locked solid in the putting stroke. With no wrist action, the stroke is a solid pendulum made up of the hands, arms and shoulders. Other players are more "wristy," as Nathan calls it, meaning a great deal of the stroke comes from the wrists. He says there should be no wrist in the putting stroke at all.

Grabbing my hands, Nathan has me press the flat palms firmly together and simulate the stroke. This has the effect of pushing the elbows out wide, which initially feels odd, but also has the effect of completely locking the wrists. My hands, arms and shoulders move as a single locked pendulum. That simple physical demonstration takes probably five seconds, but I will never forget it. The demonstration clarifies what it means to take the wrist action out of the putting stroke.

Taking the putter, Nathan places the grip between the flat palms of my hands. I have to press the palms very firmly together to hold the putter and try a couple of putts in this way. Flat palms pressed together isn't a putting grip, but it made a point: wrists locked, hands opposed. Taking that same feeling and allowing the fingers to wrap around the grip makes for a natural and comfortable putting grip with locked wrists. The grip feels good, feels solid, feels predictable. I also feel a bit of a dork with my elbows spread wide. Looking around the putting green, I can plainly see other good players with locked putting wrists and the same opposed elbows.

The last part of Nathan's putting lesson this morning is slamming in those short putts assertively. Taking a golf tee, he presses it into the middle back lip of the hole, making a small target. Now he says, "Put those putts in strongly so they hit that tee on the back of the hole before dropping in." I put a whole series of putts in, hitting harder and harder each time. It is amazing how hard one has to slam a putt to get it to whack into the back of the hole. I have the feeling, hitting that hard, that the putts will just fly over the top. Certainly, if one misses, the ball will go fifteen feet past. Once I get used to slamming these short putts it is a great feeling. Nathan says the big thing about sinking the short putts hard is that one needn't worry about the borrow. This is certainly how one sees the pros sink the shorties. Tiger does this on six or eight-foot putts.

Driving home, I had the feeling that this putting lesson had been really revolutionary. I had learned something that was going to make a huge difference to my game. I could really feel progress now. What a wonderful feeling!

On the way home I stopped in at at the Pink, only to see my own cousin thrown out of the place. He'd come in for a drink and to get some food for his kids. He was eating out at the fancy restaurant across the causeway later that evening. Just as his drinks and the meals for the children were being handed over the bar, Bill, as if from nowhere, materialized and announced that it's a pub rule that there are no children's meals unless the adults eat, too. Some dark instinct in Bill's soul knew what my cousin was really up to: his kids eat at the Pink while he goes for the fancy food. The young barman standing next to Bill had the wide-eyed look of a rabbit caught in headlights. Clearly he'd never heard this rule before.

On my cousin's face I witnessed that same look of confusion that the lawyer had a few days earlier. All around him, kids were eating while the adults just drank. My cousin made a fatal mistake: he questioned Bill and there it was - banned for life. My cousin's been banned for life from the Pink each and every summer since I can remember – he's well used to the routine.

Part of the fun of each new Bill outrage was the round of phone calls that followed. The community almost enjoyed being under the lash. Bill-haters would bay like dogs. Friends of Bill, with broad smiles, were heard to exclaim, "Ah, isn't Bill great!"

9
A Lull in Play

*T*hat putting lesson was my first "high." A major surge of confidence that big improvement could be made. Strangely, given this first feeling of success, I proceeded to do no golf at all for the next two days. We had agreed to take Sunday off, day number eight in the sixty day push. From a standing start, we had done seven straight days of golf. My body ached and mentally I was tired. It had been a lot of new golf instruction going into the head in one week. Generally the idea of six days on, one day off, is a good pattern when doing an intensive push.

Monday evening we met at Kinsale to play a nine-hole round. We found a big competition was readying for a shotgun start. Bad planning on our part, we should have called ahead. These Irish courses are vibrantly busy: young and old, men and women, all enjoying their golf. Part of me was disappointed to miss the day's golf, but an evil inner voice was relieved at not having to play. Nathan and I sat on the wall, he with a pint, me with a coffee. We were both exhausted. Late nights at Irish pubs take their toll.

It was very pleasant sitting on that wall, with the majestic view up the estuary to the sea and the bustle of the jolly mass of golfers readying for the start. A whole line of barbecues had been lit on the terrace, readying food for the finish. The smell was mouth-watering.

10
Last Round Before Nathan Leaves

This is my last day with Nathan before he heads back to London to have his dodgy hip looked at. We're moving up in the world: nine holes at Bandon rather than the shorter Kinsale course. Nathan's big plan for me today is using that three wood whenever I can. He's determined to get me back to using the woods, to improve distance. The trouble is, while I'm catching the odd good wood shot, the majority are complete fluffs, rolling off the tee forty five degrees left to be lost in thick bush. To avoid getting the woods back into my game ending up being a complete disaster for my scores, confidence and ego, Nathan says whenever I duff a wood shot I can just hit another and not count it. This seems like major cheating to me. Nathan cheerily proclaims that in no time at all I won't be duffing the woods, so it will be a non-issue. In the meantime, unlimited wood mulligans will let me relax and feel good about the game.

Nathan's seemingly boundless wellspring of confidence that my game would definitely get better was a huge part of what kept me going in those early days. It was a time of great uncertainty. I worked really hard, but appeared to only get worse.

Nathan came back to the house for lunch before leaving for London. With much hilarity he stood in the kitchen aping my performance on the first tee for the assembled throng. First, he showed my practice swing: slow, measured, head staying down. Second, my main swing: a fast snatch, head looking up before I'd even hit the ball. I know Nathan wasn't doing this demonstration for my benefit; he was just trying to get a laugh at my expense and he got a great laugh. His antics really were very funny. Actually, I found his demonstration eloquently useful. It showed me exactly what I was doing on the first tee. My practice swing was completely different from my real swing. My real swing was still far too fast and I was looking up to see where the ball went before I hit it. Nathan's humorous demonstration laid the foundation for solving my driver problem.

Over lunch the talk came around to what my expectations were in this sixty day push to get my golf game together. I was honest in my view that after ten days of hard work I was still in a state of complete disbelief, doubting I could ever make major improvement. The friends at lunch seemed amazed that I was bothering to do this if I didn't believe it could work. My response was, I was doing it because Nathan continually assured me that it would work. It was definitely Nathan's confidence that started me on this sixty day quest. At day ten, it was still Nathan's confidence, rather than my own, that kept me going.

How Am I Doing? - Day 10

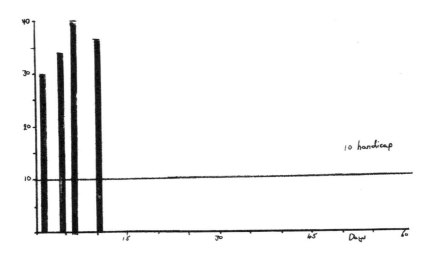

The graph, at day ten, shows the four nine-hole rounds that I'd played thus far: the first three rounds at Kinsale, the fourth at Bandon. The graph shows that for the second and third rounds my performance kept getting worse. The fourth round at Bandon, a harder course than Kinsale, shows some improvement.

The first three figures shown on this graph relate to handicap based on the score of that day. For example, the assessment round on Day One was a score of fifty, which is fifteen shots over the par of thirty-five for that course. Expressing this fifteen over par for nine holes as an eighteen-hole handicap gives a handicap of thirty.

After the first three rounds, the graph begins to report average performance. For round four, the graph reports a handicap based on the average performance of the last four rounds, i.e. rounds one through four. Graphs shown later, when more data points are available, report a handicap based on a five score rolling average, i.e., the average performance of the last five rounds.

11
The Most Dangerous Part

*L*ittle did I know, as Nathan's car disappeared around the corner of the long drive in a spray of flying gravel, that I was entering the most dangerous part of my quest, the part where I would almost quit, walk away from the whole thing. Of course, at the time, I had no idea.

It's a funny thing, but I think often in life when one walks the most dangerous part of the path it's unexpected. One thinks this part of the path would be clearly marked, big obvious monsters standing there. You march in purposefully to do battle. Instead, these sections often look sweet and innocent – sunlight dappling the green leaves of the forest, that sort of thing. Innocent as a lamb, one walks in, not prepared for battle.

Having no idea this coming week would be the most difficult part of my quest, there I was next morning on the Bandon practice ground.

No play today, just hitting balls. This is the first time without

Nathan. Grumpy as Nathan often was, it feels strange to be without him.

I'm working only with the three wood. It's revolutionary to be back hitting with woods. The main thing is just to hit as slowly as possible. The more slowly I can bring myself to hit, the further the ball goes. The weird thing is that I clearly understand that less is more when it comes to the woods, but when I get the three wood in my hand and look down at that little ball, I get a craze in the brain. I try and kill the ball every time. With each swing I repeat the mantra: slow down, slow down, slow down.

That Bandon practice area is really just a big field mown tight so you can find the balls. You bring your own bag of balls, hit 'em out there, then go pick 'em up. Three's a crowd on a practice area like Bandon; more than that and people's balls get mixed up or one person's trying to pick up while another's hitting.

What's wonderful about the practice ground versus a normal driving range is when you walk out to pick your balls up you can see what you did. The story of your play is laid out before you: fades, draws, hooks, slices, flops and those few magic shots, long and straight. It's all there to see. The pattern speaks the truth. At a driving range, where there may be fifty people hitting, there's a sea of balls out there. It's easy to hit a bucket of balls at a range and remember those four or five magic shots and forget that ninety percent of what you hit faded short right.

That first day with the three wood, walking out to pick up, my pattern of balls is right sad, laughable actually: balls sprayed all over the field, hard left, hard right, a whole load of flops at fifty feet and a few – a very few – winners, long and straight.

The humour that first day on my own on the practice ground is my small audience. As I hit away, one by one, this collection of rural codgers, each leading a mangy dog, strolls across the back of the practice ground, seemingly without fear of being hit. They gather, all in a row, elbows leaning on a wooden rail, their mangy dogs sitting in a dejected, defeated pack. The codgers watch me. Though there is no movement or comment that I can hear, I have the distinct vibe that the codgers think I am some kind of nutcase, all set up on the practice ground like a serious golfer, but scattering balls left and right like I've never touched a golf club before in my life. Who knows what they're thinking? The codgers lean on that wooden railing for over an hour, watching me hit the balls, then pick them up. They come every day after that to watch. My gallery of codgers.

It took just under twenty minutes to drive back to the house from the practice ground. Rural Ireland is a dense spider web of roads – some big, some small, some windy, some very straight. This strange web affords the luxury of always having many different ways to get from one place to another. Locals get into discussions about which way is the better way from one place to another, arguing that, "it's a little longer that way but the roads are straighter," or, "you can be held up by the cows that way but there's a grand view of the mountain."

Directions in rural Ireland can go a bit like this:
"Follow the road to Ballinaspittle, to Ballinacarriga, to Ballinascarthy, then Ballyhooleen. But I wouldn't go that way if I were you."

"So why did you tell me?"

"Now if I were you I'd go to Kilbrittain, then Killnamatra, to Killnalooda, then along to Killfinora. But if I was going there I wouldn't want to be starting from here at all."

"But I am starting from here."

These same locals outlined for me multiple ways to get from the house to the practice ground. The quickest route was twenty minutes.

When my father was a kid, none of these roads were paved and dirt tracks full of potholes made the route almost impassable in winter. As a child coming out to the coast for his summer holiday, he'd take a steam train from Cork to Bandon, then a huge green steam traction engine would complete the journey from the railway station to the coast. He remembered when the road was first paved from Cork to Bandon. For years the ten-mile stretch to the coast remained a dirt track, a team of men permanently at work along the road filling potholes. Despite their efforts, huge holes still remained that cars carefully circumvented.

Those early cars were so unusual and caused such a stir, local dogs would follow them for miles. Sometimes the dogs would form such a pack that a dog bomb would be lit and thrown out the back of the car. This sounds awful, but my Father said the dog bombs were just loud bangers, scaring the dogs and breaking up the pursuing pack.

Back at the house that evening, I got to thinking that it would be nirvana if I could just hit balls in the adjacent cow field and not have to drive twenty minutes to the practice ground. A field's a field, after all. Hopping over the wall with a club and a fist full of balls, I decided to give it a go.

A friend of mine owned this field. His family had farmed this same land for more than four hundred years. There is a powerful sense of place in these parts. Many of these families lived on the same land for centuries.

My little experiment didn't go well for three reasons. First, though the grass looked closely nibbled by the cows, it was still too long. I couldn't find a single ball I hit. Second, a lot of fresh cow pats. Third, the cows turned out to be bulls. Very aggressive. I only just made it back over the wall.

Wandering around the rambling old house that evening, two mysteries started to bother me. The first was how one got into the cellar. I'd been told there was a huge full-length cellar under this big house and I could even see tiny slits of cellar windows here and there. I love big old cellars, just love to explore them and all the strange old stuff that is usually down there. I searched all over this big house and simply could not figure out the way into the cellar.

The second mystery was the rumour that this old place was haunted. My father was not superstitious, definitely not the sort of person to believe in haunted houses. But as a kid he'd had an experience at dusk in a big old house set amidst ancient trees circled by flocks of crows, where an old lady called Red Annie lived. He never said what happened, but he was adamant that he would never spend a night in that house. Here I was at dusk, under ancient trees, flocks of crows circling in the gathering gloom. It suddenly clicked that this was Red Annie's house, the house my father would never spend a night in.

It would be several weeks before I solved the mystery of the way into the cellar, finding the door in the most surprising place. I was even more surprised at what was down there. As to whether this big old place was haunted, I would come to know more about that too.

The cow field not having worked, it's the twenty-minute drive to the Bandon practice ground for me the next day. My practice with the three wood seems the same as yesterday, right up to the point when I walk out to pick up the balls. It is immediately obvious that the pattern of balls is far tighter than the day before: less to the right, less to the left and far more straight and long. I'm seeing clear and definite improvement.

I once heard that when steering a super-tanker, one of those mighty five hundred thousand ton ships, filled to the gunnels with oil, you need to make a course correction miles before you actually turn. You turn the wheel, then wait and wait and wait. Finally, imperceptibly, the bow of the ship will start to turn. That day at the range, as I walk out and find the tighter spread of balls, is the first hint that my hard work of the past twelve days might be paying off. The great super-tanker of my golf game took many days before starting its turn. Now, almost imperceptibly, there was a turn.

As I practice, another golfer comes out and sets up shop on the practice ground, hitting balls about a hundred yards left of me. This is one of the very few times anyone else has been out here practising with me. The members of this club seem more into playing than practising. Their lack of practice doesn't seem to hurt their golf. There are some right tidy players on this course. This guy who has just turned up is really good. He whizzes up in a golf car, one of the very few I've ever seen in Ireland, pokes his golf umbrella into the ground about 160 yards out, dropping back to the tee line to hit. He's now casually, with a slow swing and tremendous body turn, plopping balls down around that umbrella with pinpoint accuracy. He makes my performance look right shabby.

Overall, I find it takes around an hour and a quarter to hit sixty balls and pick them up. One of the dangers of hitting balls on the range is a tendency to hit faster and faster. As the practice goes on, a kind of craze gradually comes over you. One can end up like the famous clip of the Three Stooges, flailing away at a pile of golf balls. Instead, it's best to take it slow and steady, hitting a few balls, then take a deliberate break. Take a couple of minutes to look at the view: the cows staring over the fence, the walls of a lord stretching down the valley, the codgers leaning on their rail. Sip that dentist's cup of coffee.

During my sixty days of golf, I hit balls twenty-eight times, for a total of around 2,500 balls hit on the practice ground. It was said of Caesar that it was debatable which was more remarkable: his caution or his daring. In similar fashion, it's debatable if I hit too many or too few balls in my sixty day quest. Strangely, when all was done and dusted, I was uncertain how much hitting balls helped, or how little it helped. Success on the range doesn't always translate to success on the course. Hitting at the range almost becomes an end in itself – a meditation. Too much practice on the range can be destructive. When one gets tired, one's grooving in bad habits. No practice can be better than sloppy practice.

For the next three days, little happened on the golf front. Looking back, this was definitely the riskiest part of the whole quest – the easiest time to quit. I did some pitching at the buckets on the front lawn, some putting in the long hallway. This was not focused work, but more like filling in ten minutes between phone calls or waiting for the kettle to boil. After all my talk, all my gusto, spending a determined sixty days working hard on my golf, I felt disappointed with myself for these flabby, wasted days, with no coherent practice.

12
Crisis Sunday

Sunday was the low point, the day my golf quest very nearly ended. The evening before, I set the alarm for six a.m. for an early morning nine holes. Awakened from a deep sleep by the insistent buzz, cold and dim outside, it was so easy to snap off the alarm and go straight back to sleep. Waking later, at eight a.m., I was burdened by tremendous disappointment.

I really felt down about the golf. Since Nathan had left almost a week ago all I had really done was hit balls twice. So much for working on my game every day. Not very impressive. I felt a great sense of failure.

My quest was still at that difficult stage where it was all hard work with little reward. I had worked hard for fifteen days but still had not managed to post a better score than fifty for nine holes on my first day. In fact, my scores had got worse.

Little did I know that I was on the verge of seeing dramatic improvement, an amazing run of fourteen rounds in a row where my score came down every time. On this dark Sunday,

I didn't know all this and I was about to quit.

Today would be the day, when I was feeling most down, that I had to decide whether to ask Nathan to come back. I had major doubts about him coming back. It would be very easy to call Nathan and ask him not to come, to quit the quest.

All day long I dithered. I kept going to the phone on the point of calling Nathan to say, "Don't come." I wandered from room to room in this big house. I couldn't sit down: out into the garden, back in the house, out, back, to the phone, almost dialling. This went on for hours. A huge inner conflict raged: do I go on with the golf or do I quit? Several times I walked with purpose to the phone, intending to dial quickly, make my excuses to Nathan and ask him not to come.

Military historians see all battles, all wars in fact, as having a crisis point, or tipping point, when the battle is won or lost. For example, the battle of Waterloo went on all day, hours and hours, but the exact point when the French lost that battle was the few seconds when the Imperial guard turned and broke.

The Imperial guard were Napoleon's personal troops, the tallest, most powerful, most feared unit in his army. When ordered to advance in battle, they had never, ever turned back. They always kept moving forward, always prevailed. That day at Waterloo, they were ordered forward, a splendid and fearsome sight. In fine order they advanced down the hill. Under withering musket fire laid down from the precise geometric squares of the British redcoats, the mighty Imperial guard faltered, broke, turned and fled back up the hill. That point, when the guard faltered and turned, those few seconds, was the crisis point when Napoleon lost the battle.

In similar fashion, Leningrad was the crisis point for the Germans in the Second World War. Before Leningrad the German army had never lost a battle. After Leningrad, the German army never won a battle.

As I wandered from room to room in that big house, wrestling with my decision, I had no idea, on this quite innocent Sunday, that this was the crisis point in my golf quest. Late in the day, I finally marched purposefully once more to the phone and dialled Nathan. His gruff voice answered. I asked him to come back. "Yes, right, okay. I'll be there Friday lunchtime. I'm moving some stuff for my girlfriend Wednesday and I'm having a drink with me mates Thursday." Click, he put the phone down. Nathan wasn't one to waste words and his whole life, work and schedule revolved around girls and drink.

In a conversation of less than thirty seconds the deed was done. I felt a mighty sense of relief at a decision made, combined with a mingled measure of dread, Oh no. What have I done?"

The very next thought was, Oh God, he's coming back and I've done no work. Once more I was the kid with my weekly piano lesson tomorrow, no practice done, one day to get it all together. At least I had four days before Nathan got back. Right then I reset the alarm clock and vowed to heed its call in the dark of the next early morning.

13
Early Morning Golf Takes Hold

One imagines the great battles in life as heroic: enemy troops coming over the parapet, one rushes forward, sword in hand. Life's real battles are much less heroic, less dramatic. For me it was the insistent buzz of the five-thirty alarm clock in the cold dark of the next morning. Answering that call, up and out on the road towards the golf course, my battle was won, the first step in creating a habit of early morning golf.

The road led up the valley and across the hills inland to Bandon. At that time of the morning not a car was about. Huge numbers of pigeons just sat in the road. The pigeons enjoyed a game of sudden death playoff with the first car of the morning. Flapping away at the very last minute, I was continually breaking sharply for fear of flattening particularly fat ones that moved slowly. In time I learned that these pigeons had it down to a fine art, knowing exactly when to flap away. From the top of the hills, there was a view to the west of huge mountains unknown to me. There is a clarity to early morning, either in the air or in the mind, that reveals new things.

At six a.m. the first tee at Bandon is utter silence. Not a soul about. Strangely, the car park is full of cars, heavy with morning dew, suggesting they've been here all night. Must have been a big do at the club last night and the members left their cars and cabbed it home. Everything is stillness.

In this silence, I set up on the first tee: my glove on, found a couple of balls, a handful of tees and out with the three wood. Careful preparation for a wonderful first shot down the fairway. Hit slow, hit slow. The swing – and that most hated result: the ball scutters left to be swallowed by a bush. With a fluid motion, I pull a second ball from my pocket, tee it up and without conscious thought swing again. This ball fulfils my earlier mental image, sailing far down the fairway to sit neatly in the middle. It is one of the most pleasing tee shots I have ever made. I was to find this a very common occurrence. Fluff a shot, quickly drop a ball and without thinking hit a second. You often get a great shot. It's switching the mind off, not caring, that seems to do it.

This is the first time I've played golf without Nathan since beginning my sixty day golf quest. The morning quickly unravels into a sense of flustered chaos. First, I seem to be continually fiddling with the multiple pockets of the golf bag looking for balls, tees, pencils. No system has developed of where things should be. Second, my intention is to keep a careful record of all my play so as to measure change and hopefully improvement. I haven't brought a card or pencil. I try to remember my score but within three holes I've lost track. A friend of mine, a good golfer, expressed amazement later that day that I couldn't keep a golf score in my head. I responded that at this stage of my game I found it hard enough putting one foot in front of the other without falling in the bushes. What was that phrase? "Can't walk and chew gum at the same time."

As I walk the course on this early morning, I feel I have the place to myself. Certainly there are no other golfers to be seen. But I know one has been before me. The ground is thick with dew. Everything that moves leaves its story: rabbits, the distinctive footprints of a fox that walked the course earlier and there, down the middle of the fairway, the lone footprints of another golfer. As I follow, this mystery golfer's game is there in the dew. Where his ball rolled to a stop on the fairway. Where his next shot landed on the green, even how many putts my mystery friend has taken.

Every morning that I came out to play I would never see him, but I always knew he was there. His telltale footprints down the fairway. I came to know him, even know how he played, as I read the story of his game in the dew. I could see the days he played well, I could see the days his game was off. My invisible companion in the early morning. In the days to come I would solve the mystery of this golfer and he would teach me something important.

The greatest ignominy, that first early morning when I played on my own, was getting lost on the course. I thought I played each hole but, finishing on the ninth, had only played seven. It shouldn't have been hard; e ach hole was clearly numbered and I had played this nine-hole loop many times before. What kind of a golfer loses two entire holes?

I learned later that day that I wasn't as daft as I thought. Cars left overnight in the club car park had suggested a party. Last night had been a big celebration for the opening of a new nine. The course had been eighteen holes for many years, but a couple of years earlier the club took in extra land. This enabled the course to be considerably lengthened and remodelled. They'd re-jigged the order of the holes, hence me getting lost. The course was now a serious layout set amidst the fat green valley of the salmon river. The daughter of the late Lord Bandon had cut the ribbon opening the new course.

This new course played past the incredible ruins of the lord's home, which had been burned in the "Troubles" of the 1910s. The IRA took to burning the Irish great houses. The night they burned this great house, the lord had been woken in his four-poster bed before they set the place on fire. Story has it, he sat in a chair on the front lawn, drink in hand, as his great castle burned. He was quite the character.
The mighty, ivy-covered ruins still stand in splendour today. One hears now about the McMansions in wealthy suburbs of America, huge houses of six thousand, ten

*"The Course Plays Past the Ruins of the
Lord's Castle"*

thousand, even fourteen thousand square feet. Two centuries ago, Lord Bandon's home must have exceeded 100,000 square feet, perhaps even twice that. In a Dublin photo archive, I recently found a series of shots taken of this house in its heyday of the 1880's. Reeking of vast wealth, everything in its hugeness was painted, clipped and raked to perfection. The European stately homes we visit today are in a state of genteel decay. The vast houses are musty and peeling, with worn carpets and flaking paint. In their day these were palaces similar to those of today's oil sheikhs or business billionaires.

That evening, down by a small slip way by the sea where the community brings its boats in, I met another of my cousins, the Jolly Banker. He's a golfer, like most of us, who struggles with his game. I told him my story of the sixty day challenge. In his jolly, happy way he just kept saying the word, "unimaginable." Single figures seemed unimaginable to me right now, especially after fifteen days of work with no improvement in my scores. I repeated Nathan's view of single figures: playing to a nine is not playing great golf; you still get to bogey every other hole. The Jolly Banker just kept shaking his head muttering, "unimaginable, unimaginable."

The Piano Player from the Pink walked down the slip passing us without speaking. Without even a pause he went into that cold cold water and swam in a direct line out to sea, way out, in a fast overarm crawl, he was a powerful swimmer.

Talk at the slip that evening was of the big wedding. Two locals were getting married at the end of the summer and there was great excitement. Irish weddings are big, with a lot of music and drink and the dancing goes on till late. This wedding was going to be the event of the summer.

Up at the Pink that night Bill was forecasting the weather again. His forecasts were famous. With arms waving and voice rising he would warn of a mighty storm coming in tomorrow. The next day would be one of extraordinary calm and peace. With equal certainty and vivid description, he would forecast a fine day. The dawn would bring a raging storm tearing the very leaves from the trees. Long-term analysis of Bill's weather forecasts revealed him to be exactly one hundred percent wrong. In a funny way this made him one hundred percent correct as long as you always planned for the exact opposite.

It turned out to be a great week for golf. I got an early morning nine holes done every day before Nathan's return. As the week went on, getting up early quickly became easy. I started waking ahead of the alarm and going out. The first day's seven a.m. turned to six-thirty a.m. on day two and six a.m. by days three and four. The earlier start brought new delights. Playing down the first fairway, the huge orange orb of the rising sun sat on the skyline before me. Prior to sunrise, the beauty of the morning mists flowed down the valleys, almost instantly dissipating once the sun rose. It was magnificent.

By Thursday I became so used to getting up and out that I found myself out on the course even though I hadn't planned it: a complete reversal from Sunday, only five days earlier, when I'd set my heart on being there, but failed. Wednesday evening, my body felt so sore that I thought it best not to play. Playing nine holes three days in a row doesn't seem like tough duty, but it left a body not fit for golf aching head to toe. Picking up an injury would scupper the sixty day golf quest, so, caution being the better part of valour, I decided to take the next day off and didn't set the alarm.

The next morning at five-thirty I was wide awake anyway. It was light outside, a beautiful morning. I thought of that huge orb of the sun that would rise down the first fairway, wanting to be out there, to witness it. Early morning golf is tough on days one and two. However, the habit rapidly sets in and sleep cycles quickly adjust. By day four, it's easy. Daily early starts are easy; sporadic ones are hard. The early morning nines were the making of my sixty day golf program.

Out in those magical early mornings was a world totally without people. I'd leave the house and drive in to the course never passing a car. Play nine holes, not see another soul, drive back to the house, again not a car in sight. The early morning light was imbued with a yellow-tinged clarity. All was total silence. My only companions were animals. The birds on the road always sat in the exact same places as I drove in. The big old hare always lolloped away as I walked onto the first tee. Two dogs watched me tee off the seventh. Cows, deep in chewy thought, stared over the walls. There were rabbits everywhere and swallows swooped low over the greens, searching for flies. An early morning world peopled only by animals.

Back in the house later in the day, remembering that glorious yellow early morning world, I'd wonder if it had really happened, or was it just fantasy?

One morning, thick mist enveloped everything as I teed off. My ball soared off, disappearing in the mist. Playing in thick fog might seem impossible but years earlier I had played golf on the slopes of Mount Fuji in Japan. The thickest of fogs draped the mountain, but nothing would stand in the way of the Japanese passion for the game. Proving this was a Japanese friend of mine who regularly played at night. She would walk down the fairway along the line of the ball, then switch on a hand torch roughly where she thought the ball was and search around for it. Back on our misty mountain, as the balls vanished in the fog, the caddies walked out on the line of each shot to discover the ball. We played all eighteen holes in this fashion. As we played, the conversation turned to the amazing views of Fuji from the course "if only it wasn't foggy," but, they went on to say, "it's always foggy here." A collision of reason only possible in Japan.

On the Irish course I copy what I'd seen the Japanese caddy doing years ago, walking the line of each shot into the fog to find the ball. I have no problem playing the first three holes in thick fog. As the fog burns off, there comes a point where the course is clear, but thick fog still boils below in the valley. One can look across the top of the fog with a feeling of being on a mountain peak, looking down over the clouds, such a magical sight.

After failing to keep score that first day out on my own, I am properly organised with card and pen the second day –a fifty-one for nine.

Score-wise the week looked like this: Monday's score forgotten, Tuesday fifty-one, Wednesday fifty-six, Thursday fifty. That fifty-six turned out to be my all-time high. The fifty equalled my first day score, but fifty on the long Bandon course is a very different story from fifty on the short Kinsale course. So by day nineteen, almost a third of the way through my sixty day quest, I still had not bettered my first day score. Wow.

Nathan gave me this simple score keeping system – simple but enormously helpful. For each hole, he said, record three numbers: total shots, number of chips and number of putts. Chips he defined as shots from within fifty yards of the green. Using this simple system my scores for the first seven nine-hole rounds are shown in the table below

Scores For The First Seven Rounds

Course	Par	Day	Round	Holes	Score	Greens Hit	Fairway shots	Chips	Putts
Kinsale	35	1	1	9	50	1	25	7	18
Kinsale	35	4	2	9	52	0	23	5	24
Kinsale	35	6	3	9	55	0	26	8	21
Bandon	36	10	4	9	51	0	20	11	20
Bandon	36	17	6	9	51	0	22	9	20
Bandon	36	18	7	9	56	0	26	13	17
Bandon	36	19	8	9	50	0	24	7	19

First and foremost, the extra numbers helped me focus on the number of putts per round. For my nine-hole games I was always looking for eighteen or less putts. Nathan had the view that for a single figure handicap I should aim for an average fifteen or sixteen putts for nine holes.

The zeros down the chips column highlighted the greens hit. The other thing my eye was drawn to was: 3,1,1 or 4,1,1 or 5,1,1 for pars three, four and fives, respectively. Those double ones meant one chip, one putt, getting up and down for par. It was saving par by chipping up and down that from the beginning had been Nathan's secret for my single figure golf.

The good news that week was that my woods were working beautifully. Nathan's unlimited wood mulligans policy worked. On Monday I had taken a mulligan on every tee, but by Thursday I was not fluffing a single wood shot. At every tee I stood there with that three wood and put the ball down the fairway with the first swing. Revolutionary.

The bad news that week? My irons fell apart. The score of fifty-six came from an inability to hit a single iron. Hitting fat, thin, shanking. Awful stuff. Painful stuff. It seems to be a reality of golf: one thing starts working, something else goes wrong.

As a child I remember the fun of building dams on those huge golden Irish beaches. The beach in front of my grandmother's house had a stream running down the middle. A gang of us would go out, each with a big garden shovel – none of those silly plastic beach spades for us – and build a dam across that stream, an earthwork almost on a scale of the Neolithic fort our ancestors left on the very hilltop above that beach two thousand years ago.

For me, the greatest excitement of dam building was the point at the end when the water lapped the very top of the dam, rising ever higher, fed by the stream relentlessly pouring into our artificial lake. Once the water could trickle over the top of the damn the end was inevitable and rapid. The first tiny trickle quickly grew to a torrent that would sweep our dam away in a mighty rush of water. At that final point, as the water lapped the top of the dam, we'd rush crazily up and down the dam looking for the weakest points and stopping to build up the wall with a few panicky shovels of sand, then run on, finding the next weak link.

Getting a golf game together is like holding that dam. You work on one area to make it strong. While you're doing this, another part of the game falls apart. Panicking, one runs up and down different parts of ones game, building up one area, building up another, trying to get all parts to work together at the same time. Hopefully, like a dam wall rising, this process gradually will raise the level of one's game.

On Thursday, with the irons in complete disarray but not entirely unhappy with my score of fifty, I retired to the clubhouse for a "cholesterol special": breakfast and a stonkingly strong cup of Irish tea. Thus strengthened, I proceed to the practice area and spent an hour working on the irons. I'm not sure this work helped much on that day, but this practice session was the beginning of a winning habit. From now on, I would play nine, take a quick break, then spend one hour working on whatever the weakest link of my game had been that day.

Today the irons didn't work, so it's the irons. Another day it might be putting, chipping, driving. There's always something not working with golf. If only, even briefly, everything would work together on the same day, I could achieve greatness. Just for a day.

14
Nathan Returns

A very late night yesterday. We drove out west for tea with friends. Driving west, everything changes. It's not a long drive, just an hour, but the scenery changes radically from the soft rounded green hills of Kinsale to dramatic mountains and bouldered outcroppings. The Irish landscape goes back to the ice. Ten thousand years ago the entire country was covered by an ice sheet thousands of feet thick, a bit like Greenland today. All this ice acted like a vast bulldozer. Back in Kinsale, the bulldozer dumped billions upon billions of tons of soil and rock to create the rounded smooth scenery. The posh word for these rounded piles of glacial dumping is drumlins. These drumlins are a couple of miles long and a few hundred feet high. In fact, if one gets really fancy, the drumlins were drowned. When all that ice melted, the sea level rose, submerging much of the ice's work, creating the wonderful harbours and estuaries that make picture-perfect postcard Ireland of today.

Out west, the ice bulldozer was scraping rather than dumping. The ice scraped the soil away, grinding the hills

smooth, plucking boulders larger than houses and carelessly dumping them across the landscape. Everything
here has a rounded, scraped beauty. In the middle of this
– the middle of nowhere – our friends built a house by
the sea. Living beside this crystal-clear, cold sea, they had
become veteran sea swimmers. In order to get my tea I had
to go swimming.

The water looked delicious; from high on the rocks you
could see deep into it. Every stone way down at the bottom was clear as a bell. My friend dove in, swimming thirty
yards out on mirror-flat water, declaring it lovely. Inching
my toes in, I found it shockingly cold.

There are two ways to get into really cold water: inch in
little at a time – death by a thousand cuts – or just plunge
in and get it over with quickly. I stood high on those rocks,
looked down into that clear, cold, beautiful water, sum-
moned the courage and dove right in.

Instantly entering a different world. Instant transformation. Cold, shocking cold, so cold it's not even cold. Clear,
still, silent. A fish surprised by my sudden appearance in
its world shoots away. Each stone of the bottom perfectly clear below me. Light from the mirror surface above.
Arching up towards that light I break through the mirror
to become a small speck on that huge flat surface.

Quickly ones body grows used to the cold. There is a feeling that can only be described as bliss, swimming the mir-

rored surface of clear, cold water. The thought of the cold is made easier by knowledge of a hot sauna waiting back at the house. Five minutes in the cold water, followed by fifteen minutes in the sauna, then a big mug of steaming hot tea. Words can't describe how great this feels.

There's a gang of people in Southern Ireland who swim in those cold Atlantic waters every day of the year. Grant you, it's a small gang. It takes courage to swim those Irish seas in the hot days of summer. To go every day into those waters through the cold, dark, wild winter doesn't bear thinking about. A friend of mine, a surgeon actually, so he can't be completely barmy, swims every day and has for years. His description is simple: at six-thirty on dark winter morning, he doesn't always feel like swimming while inching into the water, but after the swim he's always happy he did. By seven-thirty, suiting up in the operating theatre, he's the most alert man in the hospital while those around, befuddled, sip their morning coffee.

These crazy sea swimmers make outrageous claims that they never get sick, "haven't had a cold in years," that kind of talk. Recent medical research has actually shown truth in this: regular swimming in cold water strongly boosts the immune system.

It was late, as only the Irish know how to do late, when we got back. A three a.m. return from a four p.m. cup of tea. Driving back on those dark roads, I crossed early golf off my list, but was up anyway at five-thirty, awake and

alert, my body now tuned to those early starts. This time
I rolled over and slept to a civilised hour. Waking, I felt a
pang of regret at having missed the huge orb of sun rise
over the first green.

With Nathan turning up around lunchtime, I felt I should
get some work in on my corridor putting. In fact, in recent
days, I had really started to get into this. In the beginning,
my boredom threshold came fast when putting balls in the
corridor. But like many things, the more you do it, the
more interesting it becomes. I'd done a lot of work on the
corridor putting but hadn't improved. I was trying to get
to the point on the flat, predictable carpet where I could
consistently roll balls through those two books represent-
ing the hole ten feet out.

Working with ten balls, my performance to date had been
fairly consistent. The ten balls were left in a scatter from
six inches left to six inches right, with only a small number
rolling through the hole. My mind revolved around many
excuses: Maybe the carpet wasn't flat? (But then the ball
would always roll the same way.) Maybe that's as good as
you could do ten feet out? (But the pros sink those putts
all the time.)

Working hard for an hour on this putting, my mind went
back to Nathan's putting lesson. What were the basic prin-
ciples? I really concentrated on keeping the wrists locked
and eyes completely focused on the ball. Suddenly, I
cracked it! Consistently, I rolled all ten balls right through

the books. Thinking it a fluke, I picked the balls up and did it again and again. This was a stunning experience. I had cracked the putting stroke! The weirdest synchronicity was at that very moment, engine revving, gravel flying, Nathan's car hurtled up to the front door. He'd taken the twelve-hour night ferry from Wales. Fag immediately in hand, he proclaimed, "I'd kill for a cuppa tea."

There are two ways to get into very cold water and there are two ways to do an all-night ferry crossing. One way to do the ferry crossing is to get a cabin and have a good night's sleep. Another way is to spend the entire night in the bar, drinking Guinness, gambling and smoking. Nathan felt the latter method was optimal for long ferry crossings. On arrival, he was in quite a state. He really needed that cup of tea and had zero interest in my putting breakthrough.

15
The Big Fella

As we pour tea into Nathan, his animus gradually returns and with it, an interest to go out on the course. He's brought a driver he calls "the big fella" and is eager to get it going. So, out to the practice ground we go with a bag of balls and "the big fella." This is a truly enormous club. I've never seen an oversized driver before. Looking down, addressing the ball, the club head looks massive beside the tiny ball. It certainly gives one the feeling that it would be impossible to miss. Nathan hits a few balls with this mighty club. This practice ground is plenty long but Nathan has no problem sending balls fifteen feet over the top of the high wall at the back. If I could learn to tame this club, I could imagine a world of new possibilities.

By now I can hit the three wood well, but have trouble controlling that mighty Taylor-Made driver. Balls are flying left and right, all over the field. With some practice and help from Nathan, the initial erratic results coalesce into a consistently huge banana shot: not good enough to be a fade, not bad enough to be a slice. Nathan is enthusiastic,

"Nathan"

but to my eye, the shots look terrible. Nathan points out that the results are predictable, as the balls are all landing around seventy-five yards right of where I'm aiming. "We can play that!" he declares. "Just aim seventy-five yards left and your ball will be in the fairway. And thirty yards further than the three wood."

After an hour with the driver, Nathan wants to work on the putting green. He is a man with a lot of energy for someone who's been up all night drinking on the ferry. He wants to see what this putting breakthrough is all about. Nathan is someone who always aggressively pushes on to the next thing. Is this the secret of what makes him good? He can see that I've done a lot of work with the putting. I suppose I wanted him to dwell on my success and spend a great deal of time telling me what fabulous progress I'd made. He just says, "it's time to get a new putter." He declares my putter "rotten - makes alignment difficult." Nathan disappears into the pro shop, emerging with an armful of putters.

It was great fun on the putting green trying out all those putters. They all felt a world better than the one I'd been using. It was very difficult to decide which was best. Nathan pointed out my tendency to leave the ball short, so leant towards a putter that encouraged a stronger shot. After an hour with all the putters, we finally picked one and I became the proud owner of a new putter. It's definitely a great way to buy a putter, testing a bunch of them on a real putting green.

There's a thing called the placebo effect. We most often hear about this when a doctor gives a patient, usually as part of a medical trial, a sugar pill. The pill does nothing. These dummy pills are called placebos. The patients believe they've been given a proper pill that really does something. The strange thing is they often get better because their mind tells them they should be better.

The same placebo effect happens with golf equipment. When golfers get new clubs, they believe the club will make them play better, so they do play better. After a few weeks, the golfer's play settles back to what it was before. With the huge wave of technical improvements in golf equipment over the past fifteen years, there are solid technical reasons for added performance. For example, perimeter weighted heads and carbon fibre shafts make clubs easier to hit for the amateur. But behind all that technical magic, there are placebo effects. You believe those new clubs will work, so they do. My new putter felt wonderful! Placebo effect or not, those balls seemed to just roll into the hole on the practice green.

The next morning was an early nine at Bandon with Nathan. Saturday morning saw a lot more greens staff out early. Today was a different kind of day. No fog, not even dew on the ground. It was warm, hints of rain. I've been infected by the Irish obsession of talking about the weather all the time.

The number one topic of small talk in these parts is the

weather. The conversations always follow along the same lines: the hope that rain will stop and sunshine will start. On rare occasions when the sun actually is shining, the hope is that the sun will carry on shining and the rain won't start. Ireland is a green and lovely place, but it's that way only because it rains a lot. Sometimes talk of the weather can be dramatic: "We're in for trouble," "It's going to be fierce, we had it so nice." You'd think a hurricane was racing in out of the vastness of the north Atlantic when all they really mean is there's a chance of afternoon showers.

I sometimes daydream of producing a climate chart and meticulously explaining, "this is the weather! Don't you see? It rains all the time!" Sometimes I cheerily respond that I like all the weather, which I do. Irish rain is very beautiful. The annual rhythm of the storms inspire awe with their exhilarating power.

The first of the mighty winter storms come in autumn. The Irish autumn sets out in gentle innocence. Day after day of September the sea can be glass calm, so extraordinarily beautiful, peaceful and serene that you get caught just gazing in wonder. In mid-October the first great storm roils in. Within the space of a few hours the peaceful serenity of the sea is transformed into an elemental fury terrible to behold. Huge white breakers clear out to the horizon. Waves smash in on the cliffs, throwing walls of water a hundred feet into the air, to be ripped away by shrieking winds.

One time, in the midst of such a storm, I saw Mad Bill down on the cliff path. It was amazing to me that anyone would dare be down on that path in the face of such fury coming in from the sea. Soaked by the spray, his long coat flailing in the wind, arms flung wide, his mouth raging at the storm.

16
A Different Kind of Golf

That day on the first hole I put a three wood right in the middle of the fairway and then a nine iron onto the green. This really is a different kind of golf. Fair enough, I proceed to three-putt the green for a bogey, but the fairway play is great. This is the first green I've hit since the very first hole I played on the assessment round: a run of sixty-two holes without hitting a single green in regulation.

Nathan is determined that I should use the driver whenever possible. Seems crazy to me, given the massive banana shot I was doing. Standing on the tee, he makes it very simple. "Your shot's swinging seventy-five yards right, so aim seventy-five yards left – there, at the building on the other side of the road will do it." Wow! That really is playing a line. Following instructions, I aim as he says and hit away. The ball heads way out left, over the road, then starts a mighty swing across the blue of the sky, landing plumb in the middle of the fairway and a lot further up than I could ever hit the three wood.

The next three holes are long ones. Nathan has me out
with that oversized driver on every tee. Aiming way left,
the ball traverses back across the sky, ending up in the
middle of each fairway. That extra length is magical, making the approach shots far easier for me. Nathan, with that
complete confidence that so supported me in the early
days, says, "I'll straighten that driver up for you next time
we're on the practice ground." I was at the point that I
completely believed him.

Playing the course with Nathan was great. So much of golf
tuition is done on the range with the pro. You hear talk of
a playing lesson, but people seldom get around to doing
it. The biggest single lesson Nathan showed me out on the
course was confidence, a far more assertive way of going at
each hole. Without Nathan my approach was timorous.

That morning the mystery of the golfer whose game I have
followed in the dew each morning for many days is finally
revealed. Striding down the opposite fairway comes a tall
man, playing fast, filled with the joy of the morning. He
greets me with a beaming smile and a "good morning"
that you can only find in Ireland. Whenever I meet him he
can't resist passing comment on the beauty of the morning. I will come to think of him as the Happy Golfer.

In those first bleary-eyed early rounds the Happy Golfer
helps me appreciate the wonder of the morning. That first
meeting, as he walks briskly down the fairway, I stroll to
the top of an earth bank by the tee and gaze down the val-

ley. I pause to appreciate the place, the view, the day, the moment. It's so easy to rush through life, each day, never taking the time to pause and appreciate.

Before that meeting with the Happy Golfer, my thoughts in the early morning had always been about how quickly I could get it over with and get back home. After that meeting I was always happy to be out there and I truly felt privileged to be a part of those magical yellow mornings. The Happy Golfer helped me enjoy where I was rather than yearn to be somewhere else.

This morning my game feels scrappy. My irons continue to be appalling and the game a struggle. I three-putt three greens. But as Nathan tots the card on the ninth green, he calls out a score of forty-nine. Finally, I have surpassed the fifty of the first day. Nathan is very pleased, saying, he can "really see a difference." He also reminds me that Bandon is a far tougher course than Kinsale.

How Am I Doing? – Day 22

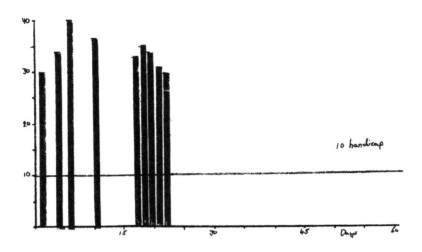

By day 22, I've played nine rounds of nine holes. The first three of these rounds were at Kinsale, the next six at Bandon. After the first few rounds, the graph reports a five score rolling average, that is, an eighteen-hole handicap based on the average performance of the previous five rounds played.

As mentioned, my average performance initially worsened after the first assessment round. However, by the tenth round the five score average is 29.6, just nudging itself under the thirty handicap clocked on day one.

17
Working Hard

Nathan worked with me in Ireland for the next six days. Intense days of very hard work. We played nine holes at six every morning, stopped for breakfast, then spent an hour practising. My brain was overflowing with all the new information Nathan poured in. My mind felt like a sieve. I feared that many of these gems of wisdom were being lost. I couldn't remember it all. Nathan was great. At the end of each lesson he would summarise the major points. I got back to the house and wrote a few brief notes on the big points, but even with this system, I felt a flow of great stuff being lost.

Strangely, in the coming weeks of my solitary golfing practice, Nathan being back in England, I found a great many of these comments that I feared lost to the wind came back. Much of it made no sense to me at the time, but as my game developed in the coming weeks, many things he'd said suddenly jumped into focus, their meaning clear as a bell and hugely helpful. Nathan, in these six intense days, loaded me with a book of knowledge, the pages of which would be revealed to me as my body and mind were ready.

For the next three days, we went out at six every morning, played nine and shot the same score every day: forty-eight, forty-eight, forty-eight. At first I was ecstatic to be consistently coming in under fifty. By the third day out, though, stuck on forty-eight every day, I felt I wanted more progress; I'd hit a wall. Nathan, exuding his usual confidence, spouted on about the way it worked. "You keep bashing away at that wall and one morning you'll suddenly go out and shoot forty-one." He said he'd seen it happen time and again. Figures like forty-one for nine, translating to eighty-two for eighteen, seemed "unimaginable," to quote the Jolly Banker. For a man who was shooting well over a hundred a couple of weeks ago and had only snuck into the high eighties twice in his life, this really was progress

Nathan would talk about anything and much of what he said was rubbish. I was, however, beginning to find out that when it came to golf his predictions often came true.

Being out early on the course each morning, one becomes accustomed to the story of everything one does being written in the the dew. I had become well used to following the Happy Golfer's game in the dew. I'd been tempted to pass comments to him like, "That was a good putt on the fifth." I felt like a voyeur, reading his game as I passed half an hour behind him.

Looking back up the fairway we had walked, my footprints and Nathan's in the dew meandered like some drunk had walked the course. It was surprising. One imagined we had walked a good straight line. When Nathan saw this he set out to walk a straight by keeping his eyes firmly on a particular tree. He looked like a right twit, striding down the fairway with his nose in the air. He did walk a dead straight line, though.

My musings about the dew reminded me of pictures I'd seen of some crazy greenkeeper doing artwork in the morning dew of his greens. During his countless mornings wanding dew from the greens, he'd noticed the patterns created by the bright white of the dew and the dark of freshly swept turf. He developed this into high art, the entire green being his canvas and created amazing pictures. The ephemeral nature of this beauty was intriguing, within moments of the sun touching the green his creation was gone.

My irons continued to be so terrible that when we have our first session on the practice ground, though I've been eager to learn the secret of straightening the mighty driver, Nathan says, "We've got to do something about those irons." This brings me back to a basic principle: "work on what's not working." This iron lesson follows another principle: when parts of the game seem to be completely at sea, return to the basics. No great magic, this lesson from Nathan: keep my head down, keep my eye on the ball and hit down with the irons. If anything, he tells me to try hitting fat, as I'd been mostly thinning those iron shots on the course.

For some reason, my leg action is working with the driver but not with the irons. I think we've all heard that the golf swing should be the same for irons as well as the driver. Why is it our brain decides to put a different swing on the clubs? I'm hitting the irons a lot better at the end of the session. I hope I can bring this improvement to the course.

Nathan does one of his amusing demonstrations, mocking my wrists waggling around at the top of the backswing. He makes me look like a cowboy trying to lasso something, club head tracing large circles. His exaggerated demonstrations are hilarious, but also eloquent. I copy his lasso thing, swinging through to hit the ball. He says I must have a good eye for the ball, being able to do that successfully. That eye for the ball is one of the only two things he said was working after the assessment round.

During the second session on the range, we finally get to the driver. Because of Nathan's confident comment a couple of days earlier "I'll straighten that driver up for you." I'm eager to learn this secret. Like most of Nathan's lessons, he starts by having me hit a few to see what's happening. He points out that while the banana shot leaves my ball far right of my aim point, the ball is actually starting off dead on aim before curving right about a hundred yards out. His diagnosis: the club head is coming through on the correct line but the face is open at impact. He does one of his slow motion swings, freezing at impact to show what I'm doing. I am astonished that the club face is that far open at impact. Is he exaggerating to make his point?

He says that to put the kind of spin on the ball that results in my banana shot, the club face has to be that far open. The driver doesn't just have an oversize head, but an oversize shaft, longer than any club I've hit. The club head has to travel much further, to get the face back square by impact. I'm not bringing the club head around fast enough.

To solve this problem, Nathan shows me something he calls casting, which involves the same feeling as casting a fishing rod. At the top of the backswing one uses the wrists to cast the club head toward the target. It feels and looks, a bit daft, as though I'm overdoing what is needed. Nathan says everything happens so fast in the downswing that if one sets out to overcorrect, it'll end up just about right. He has me try multiple, slow- motion dry runs: taking back, at the top of the backswing, wrists turning way in, casting the club head toward the target. The key swing thought starting the downswing is: cast the wrists.

The first swing at the ball using this new casting thing turns my banana shot right into a banana shot left – the complete opposite of what I'd been doing. To me, this is terrible, but Nathan is delighted. This massive over-correction shows him we're on the right track. Solving the problem is just a matter of tuning it in.

As I hit away, I throw out a mixture of banana lefts and banana rights. Gradually, as I play with the feeling and strength of the casting, the bananas grow less curved and the balls start to straighten up down the middle. This process of learning to tame the mighty driver and write my will upon the sky is exhilarating. Just as Nathan predicted, I am now hitting straight. It's incredible how much further the ball goes when hit straight. That strong fade really eats the distance off the ball. The driver, even with the banana shot, has put me further down the fairway than ever before. The driver straightened gives me yet another thirty to forty yards.

To finish up this session, Nathan loads me up with a couple of extra thoughts. First, he says, be sure to take back inside. With the longer club, I have a tendency to let it go back outside. Second, I have a habit of leaving the club face open at the top of the backswing. Both of these issues will contribute to an open club face at impact. These extras are an overload for me right now. The casting swing thought is as much as I can handle. I'll have to work on these other areas later.

18
Finding that Basement

*T*hat evening, back at the house, I finally found the way into the basement. I was exploring the outhouses of this rambling old place. One building, that I'd been in before, had a big pile of junk filling most of the floor. I don't really know why I bothered to look at this mess again, suddenly I noticed what looked like a door under all that junk. Moving some of the mess I found a door in the floor, a green door in the floor. Locked.

There was a whole mess of keys back in the house, over a hundred, mostly rusty, tied by string. One by one I went through these keys. Finally the door opened to show a flight of steps leading down in the dark.

Curious I fetch a flashlight and follow those steps down. The weak beam of light shows a long underground corridor leading towards the house. It must be fifty yards back to the house from here.

Following the corridor along, finally the basement I'd

been curious about for so many weeks. And what a great basement. A labyrinth, big rooms, corridors, hallways, small rooms, weird rooms scary rooms, dank, dark, dusty. All seemed more mysterious viewed in the yellow flickering circle of the flashlight.

Everywhere, down in that vast basement, was piled high with things left there, then forgotten, over the years, over the decades.

The early rooms where packed with furniture, chairs, tables, wardrobes, all valuable antiques, all piled down there, all broken. The whole thing reminded me of the scene Howard Carter saw when he first looked into Tutankamon's tomb. Treasure stacked right to the ceiling.

Going deeper, other rooms, one filled with wine. Looked like good stuff, old bottles thick with dust. Another room, brass cornered steamer trunks pasted higgle-de- piggledy with labels speaking of exotic voyages long ago: Mombasa, Tunis, Dar es Salaam, Zanzibar. A rail of elegant evening dresses, looked like they were from way back in the thirties, echoes of music, dancing, glittering parties, times and people now forgotten.

Deepest in this labyrinth, a final room, unusual in being completely empty. A wide expanse of open stone floor. A curious crack in the back wall. Shining the flash light in, almost looked like another room through there, something white shining back, looked like bones, were these bones, ancestral bones? This part of the basement must be under the oldest part of the house, under that ancient bell tower.

There was a completion in finding that final room and looking through that cracked back wall. Little by little, over the past weeks, I'd explored every part of this old rambling house.

As I walked back up the basement steps, a switch I hadn't seen on the way in, suddenly the whole place was brightly lit by neon strips. So much less mysterious in bright white light than viewed in the weak yellow circle of a flashlight.

Now I'd found the basement whenever children came to the house I'd show them the green door in the floor and tell them there were bones down there behind the cracked back wall of the back room. I'd give them a couple of weak flashlights, never tell them about the light switch. They would have such a good time exploring that wonderful basement.

One morning we have company. The Hurley Player joins us on the early morning tee. This is the first time anyone has played alongside me since starting the golf quest. Though he is a great friend of mine, it's amazing how self-conscious it makes me, having someone else there. This psychological block on "playing with others" will become a big problem later. Nearly all the work I do on the course is on my own and I got too accustomed to playing alone. When I start playing with other people it will really throw me. I'll sometimes play like a complete klutz.

With two decades of top-level hurling behind him, the Hurley Player has a perfect eye for the ball. His swing is unconventional, with almost no leg action, all the power coming from the forearms and wrists. Hurling has given him forearms like Popeye. He sure hits the ball a long, long way. This is the first morning I'm hitting the driver straight. I'm hitting longer than I ever have in my life. There's my ball down there, in the middle of the fairway, just a little behind the Hurley Player's. This is a wonderful feeling. Holes four and five are big, long par fours on the remodelled course. My drives put me far down the fairway, leaving just a mid-iron approach.

Nathan is all over me this morning about my short game. This is typical Nathan. I'm literally walking on air about the driving. I want to wallow in this success and I want Nathan to dwell on how great I am. He's already onto the next thing; push ahead, push ahead. My putting is bad today, three three putts in the first four holes. Nathan keeps going on that his one-eyed Granny could putt better than me. He really is on my case. He gets me so flustered I clear whiff a chip shot. That deserves a prize for incompetence.

I start feeling angry with Nathan for having such a go at me about my short game. Partly, I feel he's playing to the audience, since the Hurley Player has come along. Partly, I know where he's coming from. My short game is disgusting and Nathan's point is I am just not putting enough thought into it. He really drills into me that three-putting a green is not acceptable. I have to make an effort to really think about each putt.

19
Long Putts

As the round ends Nathan marches me straight to the putting green. I don't even get to have breakfast today! Nathan says it's the long putting that's letting me down, so it's to be an hour of that now.

To date I haven't spent any time at all working on long putts. No wonder they're bad. Nathan doesn't have any great secrets about long putting. His advice boils down to three simple things. First, you must care greatly about these long putts. Second, put serious thought into each putt ahead of time. He says I have a habit of just walking up and taking the putt without pausing to look and think. Third, practice.

He says for years Olazabal had been the best putter in the world. His putting was that good because he spent four and a half hours every day practising putting. I remember Gary Player's much repeated quote, "it's amazing, the more I practice, the luckier I get."

The aim of the long putt is to leave the ball no more than six feet from the hole. This gives a realistic chance of getting down in two putts. A six-foot circle around each hole is a huge area. One hundred and thirteen square feet to be exact. There should be little excuse for not leaving the first long putt inside that large circle, twelve feet rim to rim.

Nathan makes the obvious comment, "The more work you do with the long putt the less pressure on sinking the second putt for par." To make his point Nathan rolls a putt forty feet across the green, coming to rest two feet from the hole. He strolls across and flips the second putt in with one hand. He then marks a six-foot area around the hole, using golf tees and has me send ball after ball forty feet across the green, until every one of them rests within the big circle. Then we repeat the whole exercise from a different spot on the green.

Nathan loves turning every aspect of practice into a game. He wants a money bet, one euro per hole, on who can sink long putts for two. From the glint in his eye I know Nathan thinks he can take some real money off me here. Surprisingly, I hold my own. I never beat Nathan, but I manage to halve most of the holes. After twenty minutes I hand over six euros to Nathan. He looks grumpy. I know he had hoped to take a good wedge of drinking money off me.

Nathan's little game has made its point: leave that first putt close enough to make the second putt easy.
That evening the Doctor came in for a meal at the Pink. The

only trouble was he arrived after the kitchen was closed. Bill was a real stickler about taking food orders late. The staff were in the middle of turning the Good Doctor away when Bill appeared and handed the Doctor a menu, exclaiming, "no problem at all, Doctor! No problem at all!" The staff looked amazed.

Bill gave instructions to get the Doctor's favorite table ready, only to be told that Healy, who farmed the land up behind the Pink, was sitting at that table eating his dinner. In a tense whisper Bill directed his staff, "So move him, move him so."

Poor Healy, in the middle of his meal, was unceremoniously moved from a fine table overlooking the sea to a small corner table back by the toilet and the swing door to the kitchen. The Good Doctor, having no idea of the commotion he was causing, had a drink at the bar.

Bill came out to announce that the table was ready but by this time, the Doctor had got into watching golf on TV. It was the Open and Tiger was in the lead. The Doctor asked if it would be possible to eat at the bar. The staff looked on with interest. Bill had a famous "no eating at the bar" rule. But tonight, for the Doctor, it's not a problem. The staff now looked really interested.

Later, on his knees, Bill, the terror of the coast, served the Good Doctor his dinner at the bar delicately wielding those little silver spoons that waiters use to dish out carrots and potatoes. A gaggle of staff peered from the kitchen door in utter astonishment.

Next morning finds me battling around those nine holes yet again, Nathan plodding along beside me, smoking a cigarette and staring at the sky. Some immensely long drives. The irons are short and fading right, leaving me short right of every green. I'd be chipping each green from almost the exact same position every morning.

As we finish, Nathan adds up the card on the ninth green, calling out, "So how do you think you did?" I tell him I'm not sure? The morning has seemed like the regular old battle to me. I still can't keep a score in my head, so I really have no idea how I've done. Nathan announces, "Forty-three." Here is the breakthrough he predicted. Not quite the forty-one he'd talked of, but five clean strokes off to give the best score I ever shot in my life. While it seemed a long struggle, it is just twenty-five days since I began, five of these days I had done no golf. This morning I've hit two greens and parred four holes to get a seven over par. My putting this morning really made the score: sixteen puts for nine holes. Very respectable.

Winston Churchill made one of his famous wartime speeches after the Brits won their first big victory over the Germans at El Alamein: "For the first time we have victory, bright, clean victory". He went on to say, "Now this is not the end. It is not even the beginning of the end. But it is, perhaps, the end of the beginning."

My forty-three for an early morning nine was a victory! It certainly wasn't the end. I had a long way to go. But perhaps it was the end of the beginning. Shooting forty-three once is a different thing from doing it consistently. Seven over for nine equates to a fourteen handicap, a very long way from single figures. As I was to discover, it gets almost exponentially harder to shave each stroke off. The lower you go, the harder it is to improve.

As we took the car a mile down the road to Bandon for breakfast, the clubhouse being closed this early in the morning, I was over the moon. Nathan was his normal phlegmatic self. "I told you it would work and you've a long way to go."

Breakfast was always a welcome break between playing nine and practice. There was a wonderful little breakfast place bustling with people stopping on their way to work for a smoke and a full fried breakfast. None of the granola and yogurt types in here. Nathan and I would buy a whole slew of English and Irish papers. Sometimes, we'd peruse our papers in sullen silence. Sometime there'd be an animated debate on how we'd run the world if we were in charge. The thought of Nathan being in charge was truly scary; he had some outrageous ideas.

Next comes more work on the practice ground with those irons that are falling short and right. The longer the irons, the greater this fade becomes. The solution is casting, the same as with the driver. This leads Nathan to another demonstration that turns out to be fascinating. He has me address the ball as usual, but take the left hand off, leaving the right holding the club in its normal grip. Then I try to hit the ball. The first few are complete misses, then a few connections. I keep trying, keep it slow, keep a rhythm and I start to get the ball up in the air, thirty or so yards away. It's hard to do this, particularly for a left-hander like me.

Nathan is trying to give me a feeling of the right hand and especially the right wrist, being strong and even active at impact. A bit of extra push from the wrist. Keeping this feeling with the right wrist, but allowing the left hand back into it, there was something totally different. For the first time in my life I'm hitting a draw shot. Also, there's real added zing to my shot. If I could just bottle that all my problems would be solved. Nathan has this way of ending a lesson precisely when the story is getting good. He has just shown me something revolutionary and I want to keep hold of this, pick the balls up and hit them all again. Nathan likes to finish on a high note and also believes in not carrying on practice when you're tired. He's shown me a real bit of magic with the right-wrist thing. This fills my mind as I drive home.

20
Chipping Around the Green

Next day, post-breakthrough of forty-three the day before, I can't get anything right. I might as well be using a wet fish to hit the ball. I know enough that after a big jump forward I'm unlikely to come out next morning and break more records. It's always two steps forward, one step back. I didn't arrive at the course with big expectations, but today nothing works. It seems to be a common experience with athletic performance. There are just some off days. One tries to think: did I go to bed late, eat badly, drink too much? The mind instinctively searches for a reason. Sometimes there is no reason. One's brain and body simply don't want to do it that day. Not a single shot with wood, iron, chipping iron, or putter is working. After three holes, I ask Nathan if we can just play back down the ninth, calling it a day. Watching my sorry performance, Nathan is fine with this.

At the ninth green, Nathan says we might as well make something of the morning and gets into a chipping lesson. Pulling out a dozen balls, he starts talking about the chip shot: how one should plan the chip and figure out where the ball needs to land in order to roll into the hole. Reading the run of the green is not just for putting, but also for chipping. One figures out the correct landing zone for the chip. This landing zone then becomes the target. Nathan quietly chips all dozen balls up on the green. Each ball bounces in the landing zone he'd selected, rolling happily up near the hole. His third chip rolls right in. From fifty feet out, all his chips are within six feet of the hole, gettable in one putt. He strolls up with a putter and one by one sinks all the balls with single putts.

Nathan's chip shots end up in a long thin ellipse around the hole. The long axis of the ellipse was along the line of the chip. Nathan's view is there is very little excuse to get the line of the chip wrong. The real skill, the art, the touch, is the strength of the chip. I remember reading a book about battleships and a chapter on naval artillery. Good naval gunnery should drop the shot in an ellipse similar in shape to that of Nathan's chip shots. I suppose whether it's an eighteen-inch explosive shell or a humble golf ball, the rules of ballistics are still the same.

Nathan now sets me up to chip the balls. Having watched me for a while, he makes some corrections. Moving me closer to the ball and positioning me in a stance that is less open, he says, "The chip should feel very like a putting stroke. The hands should be light, letting just the weight of the club head do the work."

The game, it has to be made into a game with Nathan, is: to chip those twelve balls, then walk up and try to sink every ball in a single putt, just as I'd seen him do a few minutes earlier. He calls the percentages: three of the twelve up and down, five of the twelve, etc. Faced with any chip shot, one should set out with the firm intention to chip up and sink the putt. To be left with a realistic one-putt the goal of the chip becomes exactly the same as the long putt: leave the ball within six feet of the hole.

Having chipped several batches of a dozen balls from the same spot, I'm getting pretty good at that chip. Nathan now starts moving me to different spots around the green. There is infinite variation in chips just around that one simple green.

Nathan makes the point that a golfer needs a wide vocabulary of chip shots available to him. This vocabulary can be extended by the many clubs you can chip with: seven, eight and nine iron, wedge, sand wedge, plus an infinite number of special purpose chipping irons. I recently read a magazine article by the short game wizard, Peltz. He suggested that one marshal one's budget of fourteen clubs, dropping some little used long irons to add a greater variety of chipping irons. Nicklaus sang a different song in his wonderful book, "Golf My Way," the only golf book I'd ever read. Nicklaus held the view that while a pro could develop the touch with six or seven different chipping irons, amateurs should restrict themselves to two or three. Nathan took a wedge and, by opening and closing the face, he created a whole variety of shots from this one club. A wide open-face popped the ball high with a big back spin, stopping it dead. De-lofting the blade gave a long, rolling chip. A whole vocabulary of chips from a single club.

We move our dozen balls, like the hands of a clock, around that green to experience the variety of chips this one green offers. We end up spending a couple hours just chipping, chipping and chipping. Sounds boring, but it's great fun. Nathan says it's great practice, if you find a green on an empty course, to stop and chip around a green like this. Later, as I play my daily nine, with the course deserted in early morning, I will often stop as Nathan suggested, spending twenty minutes chipping.

Nathan's number one message about getting to single figures is getting up and down. The ability to chip the ball up near the hole, then sink the putt, is crucial. This is Nathan's secret of single figures. In his own words, to "chip and putt like a god." If one can get up and down, one can get away with sloppy fairway play, not hitting the greens. As long as the ball is around the green in standard, two shots on a par four, chip it up, a single putt, there's the par. Nathan always comes back to his mantra: "a nine handicap can bogey every other hole."

The point was reinforced by a memory of walking around with a ladies' tour player, some years ago, as she played the famous number two course at Pinehurst. This lady was not long off the tee, but always straight. Her approach shots did not always find the green. Methodically, she could chip up, then sink the putt. Hole after hole, she could get up and down, chipping up, then putt down. It was almost boring to watch. Bogies never happened. Every so often a birdie, where her approach shot found a green and she dropped a fifteen-foot putt, or a chip, went straight in. Without any of the fireworks of huge drives, or pinpoint approach shots bouncing by the pin, she methodically got up and down hole after hole, clocking a one under par round, on a course that was no cakewalk.

21
Last Day with Nathan

My last early morning round with Nathan is uneventful. A score of forty-five isn't a record, but for me it's respectable. The woods are now working very well, leaving me way down the fairway. With the woods working, the new long holes at Bandon give me no trouble. The long downhill par three seventh hole, at one hundred and ninety yards, used to be a problem for me. Prior to getting the woods into action, I didn't have a club in the bag that could reach it. This morning, I hit a gentle three-wood that sends the ball well over the top of the green, landing twenty yards past. Nathan suggests taking a second shot with the three-iron just to see what will happen. This shot lands the ball nicely on the green. With my new grip, the leg action and the extra zing from the right wrist, my irons are going further now. It really is wonderful to play those same holes each morning and see the balls landing further and further down the fairway. Overshooting greens: a problem I'd never had before.

Back on that tee, Nathan is now in fits of laughter. "That's classic," he says. Two dogs had been happily trotting by as

I'd been taking that second iron shot, busy country dogs with places to go, things to do. As I'd set up to take my shot, the dogs stopped, sat down and watched politely as if they too were well behaved members of the club. Once I'd hit, the dogs got up and trotted busily on their way.

We met and talked with the Happy Golfer as he came shooting down the opposite fairway. He told us he played eighteen holes every day and it took him two hours to play. At the speed he walked I'm not surprised he could get around that fast. Even watching him take a fairway shot, or putt a green, I saw that he was fast. He'd have the club out of the bag before he got there, stop, hit the ball and be off again in one fluid motion. He seemed to play well. There's so much talk these days of slow play; even with a golf car, a round can take five or even six hours. The Happy Golfer's two-hour round, walking, demonstrates a different way to do it.

Retired now, he decided to play a daily eighteen holes, early every morning, for exercise. It seemed to be work-ing – he certainly looked fit and he was about the most cheerful man I'd ever met. He said that for years when he was working he never had time to play. In fact, he'd had his clubs in the trunk of his car for twenty-five years, but couldn't recollect ever playing. He'd actually moved the clubs through several cars in that time but never used them. How many of us are in that situation? I know for my part, my clubs must have stayed in the car for five years, seeing use but once a year. Eventually they were "downgraded" to the garage, then the ignominy of the attic.

Nathan and I drove down to Bandon for a ceremonial "last breakfast" together. He was returning to England on the ferry today, a daytime crossing this time. I wondered if Guinness, gambling and smoking would occupy his twelve daylight hours on the ferry. I believe the ferry has a chapel, I suggested a day of meditation and prayer. Nathan ignored that comment as he engrossed himself in a British tabloid's front-page story about "a vicar who had stolen one of his parishioner's poodles and eloped to the South of France." It was good to see Nathan keeping up with important world events.

As we read our papers and munch our breakfast, Nathan steered the conversation around to whether I would like to buy his driver, with the subtle opening remark, "So, what are we going to do about the Big Fella?" He knew I was hooked. I couldn't imagine not having that extra distance. There was much canny negotiating from Nathan about how much this club cost in the shops, how much he liked it, the fact that his brother had already offered him such-and-such amount for it, that sort of thing. The Irish rule of negotiating is: if they ask a thousand, they mean eight-hundred, they'll take six-hundred, but settle for four hundred, so offer them two hundred. Over the next half hour, as we munched toast and read papers, the negotiation for the Big Fella moved like molasses. We settled for three hundred. Nathan looked hugely happy, so I probably paid too much. On getting home, the other rule of purchase set in, the four

prices paid: the asking price, the sale price, the price you
wanted to pay and the price you tell people you paid.
I said goodbye to Nathan amidst the busy morning bustle
of Bandon high street. He jumped into his car and drove
for the ferry, ending his direct involvement in my sixty-
day quest for single figures.

I was twenty six days into my program. It was Nathan
who started me on this quest and to date it was the constant
confidence flowing from Nathan that it could be done that
had kept me going in my dark days of self doubt. I had no
idea that I would never see Nathan again. From now on
the belief to keep me gong on the quest had to all come
from me. Nathan was out there, I did talk to him a few
times but it was hard to track him down on the phone.
I never had that solid feeling that Nathan was there any
time I needed. Wraithlike he could be found at odd moments, in a couple of gruff sentences he gave hugely helpful pointers, then would again disappear.

How Am I Doing – Day 27

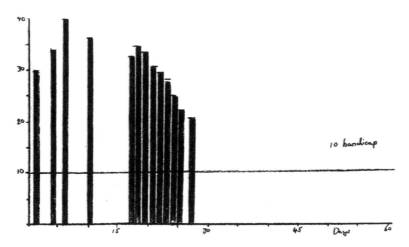

By the time Nathan left on day twenty-seven, the daily graph of average scores showed marked progress. I had now played thirteen rounds and for the past seven my handicap, based on the rolling average of the past five scores, had fallen every time I played. After the thirteenth round on day twenty-seven, my handicap had fallen to 20.8.

22
Cracked It then Lost It

*E*arly next morning, excited about owning the Big Fella, I'm up and out on that Bandon practice ground. I had one of the best practices of my life. Every ball I hit seems perfect. I hit a whole bag of balls with that mighty driver and each one seems to fly straight and long. Very long. Everything about my swing feels perfect. Picking up the balls, I feel so elated I hit another half bag down there with my three-wood. These too seem imbued with magical power. My stronger swing sends the balls flying off with a fizz I've not heard before. This whole practice reminded me of that scene in the film Caddy Shack when the player's game seems touched by God, every shot flying perfectly.

At lunchtime on that sunny Saturday, I couldn't contain my excitement. Down at the boating slip I told the assembled throng that I'd achieved a breakthrough, cracked the game. To this point I'd been somewhat reticent about telling too many people what I was trying to do with my golf. A fear of failure silenced me. I figured, if not too many people knew what I was doing, I could quietly drop the golf quest if things went poorly. My magical success that morning opened my mouth. My cousin the Jolly Banker was there. A fellow golfer, he understood my excitement.

I couldn't stop thinking about how well I'd hit the ball that morning. I wanted to bottle this, keep it, own it. The feeling led me back to the practice ground that afternoon. This turned out to be a mistake.

The mistake was compounded by bringing my brother along. I'd babbled on to him about how fantastically I was hitting the ball. He came with me to see what I was talking about and hit a few himself.

The magic that possessed my game that morning had completely deserted me. The wet fish of a few days ago returned. I looked like a complete idiot to my brother. He was quietly doing a very tidy practice next to me, methodically working up through the irons, finishing with a few woods, his balls going straight and true while mine careered widely around the field.

I did not possess the wisdom to just accept or embrace the afternoon. Instead, I bashed away, hoping the magic would return. It didn't. I just ended up with blisters on my hands. Crazed as I had become, I did possess the perspective to appreciate the transformation over the past three weeks. Three weeks before Nathan had trouble keeping me on the practice ground. Twenty minutes into hitting, I was trying to lure him away for coffee, breakfast, or any other feeble excuse. Now, voluntarily, I'd hit four bags of balls down the range in a single day and had bleeding blisters on my hands to prove it. Was I going nuts? Golf can make you nuts.

Back at the slip that evening, I was much chastened. Having made the mistake at lunchtime of "spilling the beans," people were now asking questions about my breakthrough. I admitted that my breakthrough had been rather short-lived, deserting me within mere hours. I mentioned earlier to the Jolly Banker that if this golf quest works out I might try and write it up as a book. On hearing about my woes from the range, he suggested with a broad smile that maybe I could do the story "as an unfolding disaster, a bit like Bridget Jones' Diary." Given the way things were going that evening, it didn't seem like a bad suggestion.

23
A Curious Six-Hole Course

My brother invited me to play Lisselan, a six-hole course a half-hour drive west. I was intrigued. I'd never played a course with fewer than nine holes. Sounded kind of funky. Anyway, it would be nice to get a change from the front nine at Bandon, which I'd gone around so many times.

Driving west, a soft rain began to fall as we reached Timoleague. I asked my brother if we should turn around, as it would be a pain to drive the half hour west to be rained out. He was of the opinion that the rain was light and would pass. Timoleague has the picturesque ruins of a massive old abbey standing at the head of the estuary. These walls date back a thousand years; the scale and architecture suggest a period of great wealth. The sunlight paints magical colors on these old stones, sometimes glowing golden, other times black with forbidding silhouettes.

I imagine these long estuaries being perfect for the shallow draft of Viking boats a millennium ago. Those splendid craft moored where the ruined monastery now stands.

Did they bring to these peaceful green hills the rape and pillage they're famous for?

History does show, around eight hundred years ago, that over a period of several decades, Viking boats stopped in Ireland on their way to settle Iceland. Over this period, the Vikings kidnapped around fifty thousand women, carrying them off to settle the new land. Imagine the scene. Right here, this sleepy place where I now come to buy soft-scoop ice cream: did these things happen here? Viking longships appearing out of early morning mists, grabbing all the pretty girls, taking them out to sea, never to be seen again? History also shows the Vikings had a great civilising influence. Their navigators explored vast areas of the world. They founded many of Ireland's cities, Dublin and Cork included. Did they found this small sleepy village of Timoleague?

Timoleague suffered terribly in the years of the potato famine. Government inspectors' reports of Timoleague during the famine tell of "dead bodies pulled from houses by dogs to be devoured in the street." Amidst the brightly painted, flower-decked houses of the small village today, such horror is unimaginable. Layer upon layer of history in these parts is clearly visible in today's landscape, giving the place its own vibration. This is old land and much has happened here.

As we reached the Lisselan course, the rain was coming down so hard that, even with the wipers at full speed, we couldn't see through the windscreen. It seemed ridiculous to even think of playing in such rain, but nothing could stop my brother. He's the man who plays in rain, sun, wind, or even snow.

I heard a story about the Old Course at St. Andrew's. It was a wild Scottish day. The rain was horizontal. Two old members came in from playing to take a drink in the Great Room. Hanging their soaking outer clothes by the window, where they dripped noisily on the floor, they sat in the deep leather armchairs by the big fire, sipping their drinks. One member said to the other, "Shall we play the same time next week?" His fellow member replied, "Yes, weather permitting." Weather would never stop these two old boys going out, nor would it stop my brother.

As the rain lashed the car, my brother's opinion was that it didn't look too bad. I didn't have any wet weather gear and I couldn't see that my brother had any either. With the thought that we were both in the same boat, I agreed to play. As we paid our green fee at the tiny clubhouse, my brother reached into a pocket, producing a small bundle held together by an elastic band. He proceeded to methodically unfold this impossibly small bundle until it became a complete head-to-toe set of rain gear. Now warmly wrapped, he happily walked outside to play. Before I even reached the first tee I was already so wet that my shirt and shorts stuck to my body and my shoes squelched loudly as I walked. All I could do is laugh, "Ah, 'tis a warm rain." I'm already soaked. Let's enjoy the golf.

The six holes at Lisselan are stunningly beautiful, perhaps more so in the rain. The course snakes along the floor of a perfect river valley. We criss-cross the river, which is famous for its salmon, on numerous small bridges. Just down the valley there's a little smokehouse that makes some of the best smoked salmon in Ireland. I've been told the smoked eel they do is even better, but I've never had the courage to try it.

It's interesting playing my new golf game, which has changed so dramatically within the past couple of weeks, alongside my brother. I've played golf with my brother sporadically over the past twenty years. Neither of our games changed much in that time. My brother has always been the better player. There's the usual first tee arranging of bets, prompted by my brother. One euro per hole was agreed. I expected to lose – those negative thoughts again.

Sibling rivalry is a real thing and in life, brothers are not always the biggest source of compliments. All this notwithstanding, my brother is immediately complimentary, even generous, about my game. He can see a big change. He's having to lay up in front of water hazards that my newfound driving ability allow me to fly. I really got the right-wrist-thing working with a five-iron tee shot to a par three. The ball fair shot from the club with an energy that surprises me and amazes my brother. I tell him about this "right wrist thing," but my mumbled and confused explanation sheds little light for him. My fairway play is now longer and straighter than his, but he's canny around

*"The beauty of the Lisselan course
is extraordinary"*

the greens. We remain neck and neck with the money bet. The rained pours down and my brother stays snug and dry in his copious rain gear. I'm soaked to the skin, but strangely the wetness is not a bother. The rain is warm and rather beautiful.

The beauty of the Lisselan course is extraordinary. At one point, we board a little wooden ferry. Turning a big crank handle, the flat-bottomed craft pulls itself along a rope crossing the salmon river, wide and shallow at this point. This part of the course takes you to Lisselan House. It's a small Great House, if that makes any sense, set amidst a magical formal garden. The course plays up through this garden. I've never seen anything like it.

Finishing our first loop of six holes, my brother suggests a second loop to make it twelve. For golfers accustomed to the tyranny of eighteen holes, this may sound daft, but having grown used to playing nine each morning, playing twelve comes across as right sporty.

On the finishing holes our money game is neck and neck. Today my brother is really determined to take money from me. The trash talk you sometimes hear in basketball – your Mama this, your sister that, insults meant throw you off, is not usually part of golf. My brother, to win his euro, embarks on the English club golfer's equivalent of trash talk, measured, polite, but still trash talk:
"There's a lot riding on this shot."
"That's a very tricky putt there."

"You'd better hurry; there's people waiting on us."
It all comes down to a two-foot putt on the last hole. My brother's trash talk just doesn't phase me. Having practiced hundreds of two-foot putts with Nathan, I know what to do. I slam that ball hard into the back of the cup and my brother hands over his euro. It's great, really great.

The magic of Irish weather is sudden change. The heavy rain of the day gave way to a wonderful summer evening. We stopped at the Pink for an early drink. Sitting on that patio on an evening like this, looking out over the sea, is stunning. We walked in to find not a soul in the place. As if in a stage play, Caroline, who'd worked there for years, shot out and just had time to say, "We're a bit tense tonight," before Bill also appeared, full throttle, arms flailing, instructions flying. We knew not to make eye contact. We ordered drinks and stared assiduously at our pints, agreeing with anything and everything Bill had to say.

24
Breaking for Food

*T*he next two days looked like no golf for me. My wife was set on going to Ballymalloe, famous for its cooking school and restaurant. Having started to taste success with this golf and with thirty-one days remaining to reach my single figure target, I felt a little tense letting two days slip. I left the clubs behind, seeing no hope of golf. Driving through the stately gateway of Ballymalloe, there was a small course laid out in the grounds. I could picture my clubs propped in the hallway back at the house and felt sick as a parrot.

Ballymalloe is a wonderful Georgian country house, magnificent in scale and elegance, that has been transformed by Darina Allan into a world-famous cooking school. It sounds like an overstatement, but Darina Allan single-handedly changed the face of Irish cuisine. Prior to the Ballymalloe cooking school, Irish cooking had a reputation for overdone meats and over-boiled vegetables. Today, Irish cuisine is incredible, boasting a tremendous variety of top quality restaurants. It was the graduates of the

"The Front Door at Ballymaloe"

Ballymalloe who went out in the hills, valleys and big cities of Ireland and achieved this transformation. Today, not all Irish restaurants and chefs trace their pedigree directly to Ballymalloe, but Ballymalloe was the prime mover.

Many of these wonderful Irish restaurants, Ballymalloe included, are members of the Slow-Food Movement. This movement, a reaction to the horrors of fast food, promotes the slowing down of all aspects of food. The movement holds that food should be grown slowly, prepared slowly and most importantly, eaten and enjoyed slowly.

Ballymalloe has a cooking school, a wonderful restaurant, a hotel and, as I discovered, a golf course. As we entered via the splendid Georgian doorway, my wife was tremendously excited to be here in this cathedral of cooking excellence. I was excited to see a pile of mouldy golf clubs strewn carelessly by the door, about the most rotten clubs I'd ever seen, mixed up with tennis rackets, cricket bats, old shoes and croquet mallets. I didn't care how rotten these clubs were; I could hit balls! I really had become a bit obsessed.

Rummaging through the pile of clubs, I found a rusty five-iron and an old three-wood that was actually made of wood. I hadn't seen one of those in a very long time. At least it didn't have a hickory shaft. Rowan, my two-year-old son, had also been rummaging in the pile. Finding a plastic set of child's clubs, he trotted beside me importantly, trying to shoulder his little bag, as it repeatedly slipped off him. Clattering past the swells, sitting out on the old stone patio, we looked an odd couple: me with two rusty clubs and an old bag of balls, Rowan eagerly trotting beside me with his tiny set of plastic clubs.

I have a wonderful, peaceful and very satisfying practice, hitting the five-iron down a slight slope to a lone tree 160 yards out. I'm hitting gently, but my swing thought is the right wrist. I'm amazed how much power I have with so little effort. The balls fizz away, a slight draw, landing in a pleasing cluster down by the tree. My days of scattering balls widely around the field are gone, at least for now.

The backdrop to my practice is the grandeur of the Georgian mansion, the swells on the patio sitting back in expensive-looking wooden chairs, martinis in one hand, cigars in the other. A month ago I would have been far too self-conscious to practice with anyone watching. Today, I feel fine and even proud, to be watched. The balls are flying away consistently and I feel my swing looks vaguely like a proper golf swing.

As I work away, Rowan has a project of his own going on. His game is to put as many golf balls as possible into his little plastic golf bag, then try and get the clubs in, shoulder the bag and try to walk off. Every time, the bag falls off his shoulder and the balls and clubs spill out all over the place. He happily starts again, piling everything back in the bag to do it all again.

A portly man rushes up with his teenage daughter in tow. Both carry motley sets of clubs, clearly gleaned from the pile in the hallway. He asks me where the first tee is. I reply that I don't think there is anything quite as formal as a first tee; you start somewhere around here and hit away towards that green in the distance. They hit and hurry into that green distance. The honesty box casualness of some Irish golf is refreshing after the world of seven-minute tee times, yardage books, ninety degree cart path rules and GPS enabled golf carts.

Suddenly, I realise my son has disappeared. Where could he have gone? He was here just a moment ago! We're surrounded by wide expanses of open grass. How could he disappear? An odd series of panicked thoughts race through my brain: where did he go, how did he move that fast, I've lost my son, what will I tell my wife? Walking in rapidly widening circles, I approach the gnarled trunk of an ancient oak. The massive trunk is completely hollow. In its roomy interior my son is happily playing. I remember those stories of Robin Hood and his merry men hiding in hollow tree trunks to ambush the Sheriff of Nottingham, no doubt ancestors of my son. His great-grandmother insisted she was related to Robin Hood, or Robin of Loxley as he is properly called. Her name was Loxley.

Gathering our clubs, we went walkabout through this magnificent property. An old doorway in an ancient wall, inside we discovered the Victorian kitchen garden. Neat rows of well tended vegetables, every known variety, within these high stone walls. On through a further doorway the sylvan scene of a village pond with ducks and geese floating about. The sylvan bit evaporated quickly when the geese charged us. We escape the geese, slipping through the next gate to find a tennis court. The portly man and his teenage daughter, having finished their golf, are now playing tennis. He is looking hot and disgruntled. She has a powerful game, a backhand that sends the ball low over the net with strong topspin. He can't get a single shot back to her and he doesn't like this. He shouldn't have bought her so many lessons. This man's hurried desire to do everything in this one afternoon sends me into a reverie on whether we taste more of life by doing more, or doing less?

Beyond the tennis, we discover the pool. The strong limbed children of privilege with perfect swim strokes and amazing gymnastics on the steep grassy slopes. Finally, full circle, back to the stone slabs of the patio and a drink. Not a jar of Guinness in sight round here. Champagne and martini are the drinks choice for this lot.

Dinner in this shrine of culinary excellence did not disappoint. My wife was drawn to the pig trotters appetiser. Sounded beyond scary to me. The waiter insists that "the trotters were a very popular menu item." The trotters arrive. With great trepidation I tried the tiniest of nibbles. Delicious. I wished I'd ordered my own plate of trotters. I suppose the lesson here is in a good restaurant, it's worth going for something adventurous, rather than picking old faithful menu items. The waiter asked how we liked the trotters and took this opportunity to admit that we were the first people who dared order them.

Next morning finds me out there again with the old rusty five-iron, hitting more balls out to that lone tree. I'm hoping to recapture the peace of the practice I had the day before. It doesn't happen. Today is one of those restless, uneasy, harried practices, where nothing seems to work quite right.

The next golf ball I would hit would be four thousand miles away in America.

25
A Week in America

*D*ay thirty one was lost to golf. My wife and I had a different challenge: taking a two-year-old on an eight-hour transatlantic flight. We were heading off to spend a week in the Adirondack Mountains of upstate New York. I was determined that this would not be a week lost to my sixty-day golf quest. I'd become very comfortable with the practice ground and first nine at Bandon. The challenge was to quickly find an alternative place to play and practice.

Next morning, my body clock still on Irish time, I was up far too early. I set out in the car to look at the local golf courses and find a place to play. Some courses were very private, others were very short, but one was just right. It had a driving range and an eighteen-hole course. The course, at 6,070 yards, was short compared to the 6,600 yards at Bandon that I had grown used to.

Checking in the pro shop to see if I could play next morning, I pick up a bucket of forty balls and proceed to the range. This is a proper driving range – no bringing your own balls or picking them up here. Also, it is off mats, not grass. Being used to practising off grass, the mats are a shock. I do more off that gentle swinging with the five, the swing thought still on the right wrist. With enough practice I hope my muscle memory will make this second nature. I'm still hitting that nice draw shot I coveted so much.

At six the next morning I'm driving to the course for an early morning nine. Stopping on the way, I pick up a coffee; no little dentist's cup here, but a great big honest bucket of American coffee.

Approaching the course, I was shocked by the difference. At Bandon there would not have been a soul about at this time of the morning. This small course, hidden in the Adirondack Mountains, was a hive of activity at six a.m. The car park was already completely full, busy golfers prepping their clubs, finding their shoes, stretching their backs. There was already a line at the first tee.

The other big difference was the golf cars whizzing about everywhere and long gleaming lines of them outside the pro shop. I had only seen a golf car one time in all the golf I'd played in Ireland over the previous month. I felt nervous in this new environment; I'd become used to the solitude of my early morning Irish golf.

Walking around the path to the pro shop, I enjoyed the me-tallic clatter of my spikes along the path. This simple sound brought memories of people and places from many years back when I first started playing. The voice of a man perched, gnome-like, on a wooden rail outside the pro shop cut across my reverie: "There's a sound I haven't heard for a long time." American golf courses had gone spikeless years ago. Shows how long it had been since I'd last been on an American course, clattering around confidently with my metal spikes. "Spikeless" hadn't taken over in Ireland to the same extent. I got away with those metal spikes in Ireland for a month, but they were having none of it here in the Adirondacks. The gnome found it quite funny. It had been so long since he'd seen metal spikes! This was a small pro shop with no new golf shoes to be had. Today, I'd have to play in my street shoes. This was okay with the gnome.

I scavenged for a pair of waterproof, spikeless shoes later in the day. It was well over ten years since I'd bought my last pair of golf shoes. I remember they had been fifty English pounds, which would have been around seventy dollars at the exchange rate back then. Today the shoes cost fifty dollars. We all feel inflation ticks along at two percent a year, but certain things do seem to get cheaper; long distance phone calls, air travel, computers and, so it seems, golf shoes.

While there was already a line on the first tee, there was a great discount to play the back nine. Trudging out through the thick dew to the tenth tee, I found that while the front nine was a zoo, I have the back completely to myself. The tenth is a 160-yard downhill par three over water. All that water is a bit daunting on the mind for my first hole this early in the morning. I take some warm-up swings; my body feels stiff after the

long plane flight. I flop a five-iron over that water, watching
it roll onto the edge of the green. Not a bad start to my week
of American golf.

The sun is just coming over the horizon as I tee off the second,
hitting directly into it is distracting. It strikes me that exactly
five hours earlier, this same sun came up over the Irish course.
Back there it came up huge, soft and red. Here, it rises hard,
yellow and hot from the get-go.

As I play my second hole, another lone golfer catches up
with me, riding a golf car. My new golfing buddy is a big
man. He has a great golf swing, but moves with difficulty
and obvious pain. As we chat, I find out he has a major back
problem and is due to have an operation next week. Lifting
his shirt, he shows me his back. There is a scar from a previous operation, but what's more shocking is his entire back
is bruised from whatever is not working inside his spine.
He says the doctors told him not to play in this condition.
He goes on to say he's an eight handicap, really loves his
golf, but is nervous that after the next operation golf will
be over for him. He wants to get a few last games in. I am
struck by the insane hold that golf can have. Every time he
takes a swing after that, I imagine some errant spinal disc
coming loose and rendering him permanently disabled. It
was hard to watch. With all his pain and all his bruises, he
scores far better than I this morning. I hope his operation
worked and he is playing out there somewhere today.

I find the going tough that morning. I'm not used to the humidity; my clothes are sticking to me as I trudge down the fairway. Lighter clothes will sort that next day. A cloud of midges circles my head as I set up for each shot. Fly spray will sort that next day. My street shoes are soaking wet in the thick dew. A brand-spanking new pair of waterproof spike-less shoes will sort that next day. But here today, sweating, surrounded by flies, with wet shoes, I feel miserable. I miss the cold early morning beauty of Ireland.

Misery breeds misery. My score is rotten: forty-five with twenty putts for a short nine. The greens will take some getting used to; they're fast, much faster than Ireland. One big difference: this course has all the greens freshly cut and swept of dew by six a.m. An army of greens staff work ahead of us. The U.S. greens staff ride proudly on gleaming, expensive-looking red Toro machines. This is a far cry from the clattering, smoke-spewing steeds ridden by their Irish counterparts. In Ireland I had grown used to the challenge of putting greens thick with dew. Slow, slow, slow. Some days, the challenge was compounded by some of the greens getting cut as I went round. A rapid change of gear was required to putt the first five greens uncut, heavy with dew and the next four, freshly cut.

Playing back across the lake on the last hole, as I cross the bridge, I see the enticing hints of myriad balls glinting up through the water. It must be the tinker in me, but I find it hard to walk past a water ball and not try to pick it out. My golfing buddy, riding his golf car, speeds ahead on this last hole; he has work to get to. I have a jolly time picking balls from the water using a wedge and nine iron, almost in the same way that Bill uses his little silver waiters' spoons to pick up carrots and potatoes.

The lake is home to the biggest frogs I've ever seen. Sometimes a ball seems almost perched on the nose of a frog. The big green monster won't bother to move as I fish the ball out. As always, finding balls cheers me, a palliative to lacklustre golf. You never find balls lying around in the lake of an Irish course. Back there the lakes are picked clean. I suppose America is the land of plenty, plenty of golf balls, so no need to pick them out of the water.

It is hot in these parts. Rather than follow my Irish custom of breakfast after nine holes, then back for an hour of practice, I come back to hit balls later in the day when things are cooler.

When I get back to the range I buy a bucket of ninety balls and set about to really sort out my driver. With a "no pain, no gain" attitude, I decide that if I do some really hard work with the driver, I'll start hitting the draw shot I so covet. This is a terrible thing to do. I hit that whole ninety-ball bucket. My practice gets faster and crazier and the results get worse and worse. By the time I finish flailing away with the driver, I feel weird, to the point of having a headache.

This crazed practice had an awful effect on my driving. My driver had been nicely predictable. Not as long as I would like. Not the draw that I would like, but nicely, usefully, workably predictable. After this practice my driver became erratic and started getting me into frequent trouble. It took a week to get the results of this rotten practice out of my driving and recover my nice predictable zone.

This destructive practice was the beginning of an understanding: less is more when it comes to hitting balls. From then on, I made a point either not to practice the driver on the range, or certainly drive no more than ten balls. Gradually I came to see that if this was true for the driver, it was true for the other clubs, too. Just hit a few balls with each club. Hitting too many balls tires the body and the mind. Worse, you're grooving in bad habits. The myth of beating balls to get a great game is flat wrong.

Every evening I hit balls at that range during my Adirondack week. I loved the solitude of hitting balls on the Irish practice ground as the cows gazed at me over the lord's wall, but I did find it refreshing practising in the company of the other golfers at the Adirondack range. By this stage I didn't feel so embarrassed about the state of my own game. Also it was interesting to see what the other golfers were doing.

One thing stood out. These are called "driving ranges," and that is pretty much all you see people doing: banging away with their drivers, getting the ball to go as far as possible. After my destructive experience of doing too much with the driver at the range, I'd taken to practising my irons, with a focus on trying to be predictable and accurate using my wedge nine and seven. I'd sense these guys up and down the line with their big drivers, looking at me like some sort of patsy working away with my puny seven-iron.

One evening a group of guys with little or no golf experience rolled up. It's great to see people getting their first taste
of golf. You have to start somewhere. The range lent clubs to
beginners. There were two large dustbins; one full of the most
rotten, rusty drivers the world has ever seen, the other, full
of similarly rotten irons. These guys all picked drivers. They
were big guys.

The big guys started competing with each other to see how
hard and how far, they could hit the ball. Each shot was followed by loud shouts of, "How far did that go?" And, "can
you see it?" I could see them looking across at me with dis-
dain as I worked away with my seven iron.

That evening I was actually having a major breakthrough with
my seven. I was hitting predictable shots 145 yards straight,
the balls all landing in a pleasing cluster. To the big guys, my
shots are not going as far as their shots, so I seem useless. To
them, it's all about distance.

The big guy right next to me apes the motion of a baseball
player tapping the plate. Before each shot, this guy bangs the
ground with his driver, raising a small cloud of dust. He's con-
necting with the ball something huge, but he's hitting a vicious
slice. I can't help but notice that he has the ball placed more
than a foot out front of his left foot. I suggest he bring the ball
back in front of his left heel. He tries this and his slice is cured.
He hits a huge, long, straight shot. A sad state of affairs: me,

thirty days out from being a complete duffer myself, giving pro-bono teaching tips at the range. These ex-baseball players get great results when they turn to golf. The golf swing is similar to the baseball swing, just more upright.

Part of "the thing" down at the range seemed to be the macho driver discussion. These highly stylised discussions have set kabuki-like components; noticing the other guy's driver, swapping clubs, examining the club, hitting a few balls, stating how impressed one was with the power of the club, commenting on the price and where it was obtained.

This obsession with the driver at the practice range had me pondering the over-sized place the driver seems to hold within a golfer's psyche. Has the driver, the most powerful weapon in a golfer's bag, in some way filled the psychological niche that used to be filled by the sword?

I watch my son play, he finds a stick, then runs around doing battle, fighting the trees, fighting me, fighting the air itself. I realize there's something about a good stick that resonates at a deep level. This same resonance explains our fascination with the steel stick that is a sword or the steel stick that is a driver.

The sword has always occupied some important space in the hearts and minds of men. Rich mythology surrounding the sword goes back to the earliest of times. The oldest surviving book written in the English language is the epic poem Beowulf, which talks a lot about swords. At one place the poem gives us twenty lines to introduce a sword, richly telling of its heritage and past exploits. The actual battle is then covered in two brief lines. For example, as Beowulf goes to fight Grendel's mother, a large monster who lives at the bottom of a deep lake, he is thrown a sword. The sword has this wonderful description:

Handed him a hilted weapon
A rare and ancient sword named Hrunting
The iron blade with its ill-boding patterns
Had been tempered in blood.
It had never failed the hand
Of anyone who hefted it in battle
Anyone who had fought
And faced the worst in the gap of danger
This was not the first time
It had been called upon to perform heroic feats

Throughout history and across many cultures, swords had names and personalities. They were often thought to possess great power. For example, Celtic mythology has wonderful swords with wonderful histories, such as Caladbolg, or the lighting sword, that the warrior Fergus MacRoich used to cleave a hill in two, creating a valley through which he escaped. The Arthurian legend has Excalibur, forged on the Island of Avalon and eventually thrown back to the Lady of the Lake.

For the Samurai, their swords had meaning beyond that of just a weapon. These swords had powers and lives of their own and were imbued with mystical significance. Myth has it that the first Samurai sword was made by the god Isanagi to kill his own son. Isanagi was angry with his son for the birth pain he caused his mother. The pain made Isanagi's wife creep away to the underworld, thus abandoning the god. Isanagi's ancestor was later given this sword when he came down to rule the earth. It was the first sword to arrive in Japan.

More recently, Tolkien's The Lord Of The Rings features great swords with names like Glamdring, Gurthan and the famous Narsil, broken but re-forged and renamed. The sword Anduril is described as:

Most powerful
Most feared
Most famous
Forged from a piece of meteorite
In the first age of the world

The enduring power of the sword myth is clearly in evidence in the pile of Lord Of The Rings swords in the toy department of Target and in my two-year-old son's glee in owning such a blade as he charges around, brandishing it.

Are the oversized drivers that sit in our golf bags today filling the sword myth in our subconscious? There are clear parallels. The sword myths always involve naming the sword and imbuing that sword with great power. Today, we have names for our drivers and we believe them to be powerful. It is interesting that so many drivers are named after weapons. For example, the famous "Big Bertha" driver is named after a mighty German howitzer designed to lob shells over the English Channel during the First World War.

Does the sword myth inside our driver distract us from getting better golf scores? Certainly on the driving range golfers spend more time with the driver than any other club. When playing, it's a big thing whose tee shot is that little bit further down the fairway, but those few extra yards make very little difference to the golf score. Striving for those few extra yards often gets us in trouble.

Nathan said right at the start of my golf quest, "Single figure golf comes from the chipping and putting." We have all heard that old phrase "drive for show, putt for dough" so many times that we don't hear it any more. The phrase has become worn out with overuse, but truth often stares us in the face. The short game is where the score comes from and our psychic fascination with the driver distracts us and holds us back, making us focus on the wrong thing.

For the next week, while I was in the Adirondacks, I played nine holes each morning. I came to know and love the back nine of that Adirondack course. The humidity and midges ceased to bother me. One good morning my score fell to thirty-eight! This was the first time I had ever broken forty for nine holes of golf. That morning I hit four greens and had sixteen putts for the nine. This breakthrough came with one birdie, three pars and five bogeys. The respectable score, but five bogeys, underlined Nathan's view right at the beginning: "You don't have to be a great golfer to be a single-figure player. You can still bogey every other hole." It's keeping the double bogeys out of the game that really helps.

My irons were very short. Right now my nine was not even reaching one hundred yards. With the eight missing I was often pushed up to the seven to make even short approach shots.

It was interesting how my seven-iron was stopping much better on these American greens. My iron play was not powerful, definitely nothing of the high iron shot with a fizzing back-spin that could stop dead on a green. On the rare occasions that my irons found a green the ball would often roll off the back. The longer the iron, the harder I found it to hold the green.

My longer irons: five, four and three, were at least airborne these days. The days of scrubbing them along the ground were behind me, but they weren't pretty. They tended to be short and fade right. It seemed I aimed further and further left to compensate but still ended up in the same position, chipping in from short right of each green. It would be a real shock if I were chipping onto the green from any other direction.

My chipping remained awful. I had to get to grips with

this somehow but didn't really have a plan. That one-eyed granny of Nathan's was still chipping better at this stage. The good news was that my long putting was at last showing some improvement. There was no miracle in this progress. I had finally started to spend just a little time practising the long putts and improvement quickly showed. Each time I completely fluffed a long putt, I'd go back and repeat the shot four or five times.

I remember seeing two baby deer gambol across the second fairway. I remember sitting on a bench on the fourth tee, sipping the bucket of coffee, looking way across the valley at a dramatic mountain ridge set about with wisps of morning mist. I remember seeing a heron standing very tall in a mirror pool of water, perfectly copied by its reflection. An image so faultless, if painted, it would not be believed.

One morning the irrigation system is still running. This course doesn't have fairway irrigation, just greens and tees. One by one each set of sprinklers around the course fires off, puppets dancing to the tune of a hidden control system. My progress around the course almost exactly coincides with the sprinklers. As I reach each green the big sprinklers start swinging their wide arc of water. I imagine some mischievous operator peeking out of a window somewhere, laughing, "There he is on the seventh, let's wet him down!" It becomes a game to drop the bag, run into the green and try to get the putts in before the huge sprinkler circles around to soak me. I sprint from the green as the water nibbles my heels – laughing.

The ninth is a par four. A slight dog leg left, with a tee shot over water and over high trees about a hundred yards out. I look forward to this tee shot each morning. My driving is still erratic, but for some reason, each morning on this tee, I hit the most perfect shot. The ball rises easily over those trees, hanging against the blue sky, then dropping out of sight. As I walk up, I discover it sitting deliciously in the middle of the fairway, leaving me an easy nine, or even wedge some mornings, into the green. Why is my drive always so good on that hole? Is it that I'm warmed up by then? Is it psychological? I always expect to hit a good drive on that tee.

One evening my wife and son come with me for nine holes on an aptly named course, "Top of the World." This course, high on the mountain, first opened back in the 30s, has an extraordinary view down Lake George and up to the heart of the Adirondack Mountains. They were in the process of building a second nine holes, taking the course to eighteen. It's interesting to see the new course in progress, the tantalising shape of new holes cut through the trees, big piles of sand that will become greens.

To get my two year old around the course in any kind of order, a golf car is vital. This is the only time I use a golf car that summer. Rowan finds this car wonderfully exciting and of course, he wants to drive. Once out of sight of the clubhouse we give him the wheel. Down one wide fairway he steers in wild loops and swirls. A group playing up the opposite fairway look across with astonishment.

Playing with a two-year-old brings new challenges. While I'm setting up to swing, Rowan importantly takes his own little club out to take a shot. He ends up becoming engrossed in the act of balancing his ball on a tee, never getting around to taking a swing. There is a constant risk that mid-swing he'll run towards me and risk getting hit. An added challenge: watching out for a toddler's charge.

For general entertainment, I try some shots with his tiny club and get surprisingly good results. The club is only two feet long but I have the ball going a hundred yards. I feel my swing must be pretty sound to get this strange tool to work for me.

For a two-year-old, sand traps are just huge sandboxes. As I play a sand shot, my son builds a sandcastle. As I start to rake the trap he runs wildly around it, leaving footprints and more raking everywhere as I chase him around trying to get him out.

Taking a toddler on the golf course sounds a bit mad, but was great fun. Not something you'd want to do with anyone else around. It's got to be a good thing giving a kid an early exposure to a golf course and show them it's fun, not stuffy. It's hard to concentrate though; I don't keep a score on this round and I'm sure it's terrible. I birdie the ninth. A lucky wedge shot leaves a six foot putt, which I sink. It's a great feeling driving home when you've birdied the last hole.

Next day I realized that during the fun and confusion of having my son on the course I'd left my three-iron on a tee. Going back, I found no sign of the club and it hadn't been handed in. My set of irons was fast becoming a gap toothed smile; the eight and now the three, gone. Inquiring about the cost of fill-in clubs for this ancient set of Pings left me in a state of shock. I decided to leave the gaps for now and treat myself to a new set of irons sometime soon.

At the end of our Adirondack week, I played a last early round of golf ahead of flying back across the Atlantic to Ireland that evening. As I took in the view on the fourth tee, a lone golfer caught up. It turned out the guy was from Ireland. Come all the way to an obscure little golf course in the Adirondack Mountains and you can't get away from the Irish. I have a theory that it matters not what far-off nook of the planet you take yourself to, when you get there, you will end up finding either an Irishman or an Australian. This early morning I'd found an Irishman. Like many of his race, he was a good golfer, with a swing grooved in during his teens. Wish I'd done that. Now with young kids to get back to, he looked out across the course as he raced in an early morning nine and said wistfully, "this is my golf."

As we played the last six holes together, the sky became filled, completely filled, with hot air balloons. Hundreds of them, all shapes, all colors, floating in the utter stillness of the cold morning air. It was a wondrous site, surrealistic in its improbability, but real for us on this cold, clear morning. It turned out the largest U.S. balloon festival, other than the huge one which meets in Albuquerque, was staged at a small nearby airport. As we left later in the day, we stopped by to ogle the spectacle of hundreds of huge colorful balloons being readied for an evening ascent. The roar and smell of burners inflating massive multicolored envelopes left an indelible memory as we started our journey back to Ireland.

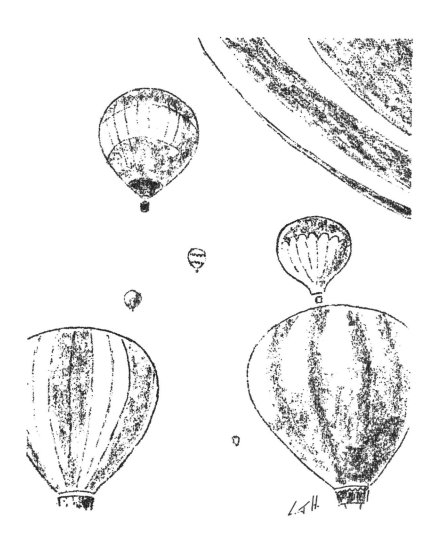

*"The Sky Became Filled With Hot
Air Balloons"*

How Am I Doing – Day 39

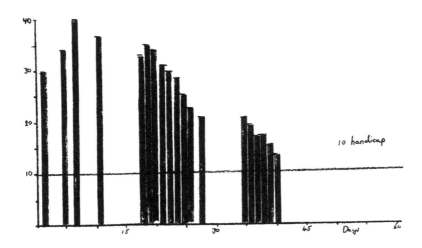

Over the past two weeks, based on the rolling average of my last five rounds, my handicap has fallen from 22.4 to 13.2, an amazing reduction in such a short time.

At this stage, progress in the score comes quickly. I had reached a point when the fairway shots were finally working. I was getting the ball off the tee, down the fairway and around the green in standard. When this happens there will be a sudden drop in the score. One thinks of progress in golf being linear, a gradual improvement in the score as the game improves. I found progress came in jumps, as different parts of the game began to work.

26
Only Twenty Days Left

*T*he day after the balloons, there I was, back on the Bandon practice ground in the soft, green hills of Ireland. This was now Day Forty of my sixty day quest for single figures. My handicap currently stood at 13.2. I had exactly twenty days left to reach my goal of slipping under ten. While my handicap had fallen nine strokes in the past two weeks, I knew that the next 3.2 strokes, to get under ten, were going to be difficult. It gets harder and harder to take each stroke off a golf handicap the lower you go.

On the Bandon practice ground, the lord's walls still stretch straight and the cows still gaze over the fence. There is a strange disconnect with jet travel; to play golf in one continent, then next day be casually hitting balls four thousand miles away on a different continent. Two hundred years ago, the simple overnight journey of the night before would have taken weeks in a sailing boat with a big risk of dying of fever or scurvy!

Fever or scurvy I did not have, but I was exhausted as I hit those balls. Flying east against the clock is always harder than flying west. Trying to get a night's sleep in an economy seat, your knees around your nose, is a challenge for me usually overcome with a couple of gin and tonics. Trying to sleep on a plane with your two–year-old son sitting next to you is even more challenging. He was so excited about the plane flight that he had no intention of sleeping. My wife and I tried pretending to be asleep, hoping he would get bored and go to sleep himself. For us, pretence gave way to reality and we slept. On waking we found our son had been up all night. The children on the left had lent him a bunch of toys, which were piled high in his empty seat. He was now across the aisle to the right playing with some other kids. Clearly for him it had been an all-night party.

No great shakes with practice today. It's hard to see the ball when your head's swimming with tiredness, but good to get a stretch after the cramped flight. I set my intentions firmly for an early morning round next day.

Back at the old Georgian house that evening I was meditatively putting in the long corridor. The corridor had become a friend. My time spent putting balls along the carpet, as the ancestors gazed down, had become peaceful interludes. I had missed my corridor. I was glad to be back.

The peace of my practice was broken by the clanging of the big brass bell out by the front door. Opening the door, I was dazzled by the lady who stood there. Her clothes were more neatly pressed, her long red hair shinier, her smile whiter and her nails more manicured, than was normal in these parts. It was the American Girlfriend. I had heard talk of her coming. She was going out with one of the local lads and had come to visit Ireland for a couple of weeks. Her visit was causing a considerable stir in the community. I could see why. They don't see the likes of her in these parts very often. It was like having a film star in our midst.

She had come to ask my advice on what she should go see while in Ireland. I can't think why she picked me to be her travel advisor. I really am useless at knowing the best things to go look at around Ireland. I've always thought this bay we are in is so stunningly beautiful, why go anywhere else?

I think the American Girlfriend thought that, as I came from Ireland, but now lived in the States, I would understand what she needed to see. She viewed me as a kind of cultural attaché. Anyway, here she was on my doorstep holding a pile of what looked like every guide book of Ireland one could buy.

I can't stand looking through guide books, but really didn't have a choice, so I invited her in by the fire, where she laid all the books out on the table. Every book had been meticulously highlighted with yellow marker to show the things she wanted to see. My immediate reaction was that it was totally impossible to see all those things in two weeks

Sitting down with her and looking through those books I

learned a great deal about Ireland that was completely new to me. There were some great things right here in the bay I loved so much that I never knew existed. Someone can come from afar and help you see something for the first time that's always been right in front of you.

That evening at the Pink, sitting with a large group at the tables, Bill was hovering, picking up glasses. The Jolly Banker, in his loud booming voice, called out, "Bill, you need to sell this place! It's getting in the way of your lifestyle." Stunned silence from around the table. Even music from the piano stopped abruptly, the Piano Player looked across, a strange look on his face.

Everyone knew the Pink was for sale, but it was a party foul to talk about it openly. Bill's only response was, "would you be passing those glasses up to me, lad?" Quizzical looks around the table. There seemed some secret knowledge between Bill and the Banker. Was the Jolly Banker bidding on the Pink?

Bill went off to do the proprietor thing, walking around the restaurant to see if people were enjoying their meal. I heard him ask one diner, "how is your steak?"

The diner answered, "well, actually, it's a bit tough tonight, Bill."

"Well, if that's how you feel, you can leave," answered Bill The poor man was ejected, his family filing meekly out behind him. Bill carried on around the room and everyone else was eager to express how great the food was.

Sometimes of an evening Bill would get to talking about his training in hotel and restaurant management, how he in fact went to the finest school in the world for this sort of thing and that some of his classmates managed famous five-star hotels out in Asia.

Six o'clock the next morning I'm back on the first tee at Bandon. That huge orb of red sun is just coming over the horizon. I can see the Happy Golfer's footprints in the thick dew, weaving their way down the first fairway. I know he's out there.

I par the first four holes. I've never done that before. I'm not hitting the greens, but I'm down the fairway and around the green in standard, then chipping up and putting down in grand style. This is just what Nathan said I would learn to do forty short days ago. After this great start, I proceed to bogey the next four holes. One of my big problems is maintaining concentration. I'll often start the first few holes with my head together and then the slightest thing will knock my concentration.

For me, early in my golf quest, the most obvious loss of concentration was what I though of as disaster holes. I'd be going round bogey, bogey, par, bogey, then BANG, a ten. These disaster holes pretty much happened the same way every time: one bad shot, followed by feeling flummoxed and rushed, leading to a cascade of terrible golf. Once it had happened the disaster hole could easily carry forward, hole by hole, to a disaster round.

As my game improved, the disaster holes had become fewer, but it was still clear to me that concentration was my big issue. When I was really thinking about each shot, my game was far better than when my mind fussed about other, often irrelevant, things.

One hears you should keep your mind completely in the shot you're doing, not dwelling on past shots you've made, or worrying about future shots. Tiger was once asked, "what were you thinking about walking up to the eighteenth green at Augusta, twenty one years old, about to win your first Masters by a twelve shot lead." He replied, "I was thinking I left myself a difficult six-foot putt." His mind was not in a whirl about the momentous occasion. He was completely focused on that next shot. There's a lifetime of sports psyche right there in Tiger's simple answer.

In yoga, there is a Sanskrit term called santosha, which essentially boils down to the same thing Tiger said. It means being in the present. When doing a yoga posture, you should be in that posture, not thinking about the postures you've done or the postures you're going to do. There is a phrase, "peace in the posture." When I was new to yoga, this phrase seemed a joke to me. You've twisted yourself up into an impossible position, it's really painful and you're supposed to feel peaceful? As I did more yoga, the wisdom of this became apparent. The postures are hard. They are supposed to be hard. However hard they are, if you stay present in the posture and relax, the posture ceases to be difficult.

The yogis have an amusing saying: "The mind is like a drunken monkey bitten by scorpions." This refers to the habit our minds have of being filled with a train of thoughts, jumping from one thing to the next. The more you can still your mind and keep your thoughts on what you're doing right now, the better it is. Whether doing a yoga pose or hitting a golf ball, stilling the mind can be the hardest thing to do.

Marcus Aurelius ruled Rome at the zenith of the Empire's power. Rather than occupying his time with hedonistic pursuits and throwing people to the lions, like most of the other Roman emperors, he devoted his life to really trying to be be useful.

The Roman emperor ruled the entire known world and comprised all branches of government in one man. It would be like the United States President of today combining the power of the Presidency, the Supreme Court, Senate and Congress, ruling almost the whole planet and never needing to run for re-election. Those Roman emperors had a lot of power. No wonder so many of them went barmy.

Marcus Aurelius did not go barmy. Instead he left us with a little book of meditations, a daily diary of what this Roman emperor was thinking about. A simple comment in this diary really stands out: "All a man can truly possess is the present moment." Here was a man of immense power, unimaginable wealth and yet he said the only thing he really owned was the present moment in time. In the hurly-burly of modern life, it is peaceful to come back to that two-thousand-year-old thought of a Roman Emperor.

"All you really have is the present moment." This thought, from so long ago, is very relevant to golf today and exactly echoes Tiger's comment at The Masters and the yoga concept of keeping the mind present.

When I get nervous or lose concentration, I speed up. I don't take the time to think about the shot or set up properly. It's counter-intuitive. When in a difficult spot, one should slow down and take more time. Speeding up when in trouble is a basic part of human nature. I play the piano and often find myself speeding up when I get to a part I'm nervous about.

Surgeons have the same problem. These days many operations are videotaped for training purposes. Analysis of the videos show that when surgeons get nervous, or things start to go wrong, they speed up. That's when mistakes happen.

A few years back, I was talking with a sports psychologist who specialised in working with golfers. He explained one of the key areas he worked on were the thoughts that go through a golfer's head during the swing set-up. He said it is critical for a golfer to have a standard swing set-up. The player should go through the exact same physical actions every single time they take a shot. If someone was videotaping every swing the player takes, the video should show precisely the same routine on every shot, from the moment the golfer steps forward to address the ball, to the end of the backswing. No variation.

This standard set-up should also be inside the head. If there were someway to make a tape recording of the golfer's thoughts every time they take a swing, that tape should record the precise same set of thoughts with every swing.

Each golfer's swing set-up, actions and thoughts, as they address the ball will be individual to them. There is no standard set-up that is right for everyone. As Monty Python's Life Of Brian taught us, "we're all individuals." The sports psychologist said that his job was working with the individual golfer, finding the set of thoughts that worked for that player. He talked about people being left-brain or right-brain thinkers. Different sets of thoughts tend to work better for left-brainers versus right-brainers.

The sports psychologist regaled me with detailed, by–the-second timing of the top pros' swing set-ups. Apparently, if you take a stop watch to televised coverage of the tour players, click the watch as they step forward to the ball and click it off at the end of the back swing, you'll find that top player's swing set-ups take precisely the same number of seconds every time. Each top player has his own predictable timing. He reeled off the swing set-up times of leading tour players.

Apparently, Norman's swing set-up was one of the longest on the tour. I think he said something like twenty-seven seconds. He cited that famous Masters' when Norman had a big lead over Faldo going into the last round. Norman's play collapsed on the back nine. Timing Norman's set up for each shot showed the consistent twenty-seven second set-up right to the collapse, when the set-up fell to seventeen seconds for the rest of the round. Norman had abandoned his standard set-up and, in his crisis, was rushing.

All this sums up to the same simple message, keep your mind on the shot you are playing and don't rush when the going gets tough. One can even make a point to deliberately slow down.

I'm out at Bandon early in the morning once again. My game is almost a repeat of the day before. The round starts with my head well together, three pars in a row. I actually hit the first two greens, the third a neat chip up and putt down. There had been a big rain the night before and the course squelches underfoot; a couple of my shots plug in the damp fairways.

On the fourth tee another lone golfer catches up with me. I've been playing along pretty slowly. He offers to join me and it seems rude to say no. In the past, faced with similar offers, I had often mumbled something about practising, hence playing very slowly and encouraged would-be playing partners to go on ahead. But my game has improved to the point that I am no longer embarrassed to play with people. Also, I've done so much golfing alone, I think it will do me good to get used to playing with people.

My playing partner completely throws my concentration. After a strong first three holes I proceed to bogey every one of the last six. My fellow golfer is not an intimidating player. He isn't pushing to play fast and he's a joy to talk to. But I am so used to playing alone, the mere presence of another player knocks my concentration. Driving home, I feel I really must work on this. Playing alone has been a great way of getting my game moving forward, but now I should make a point of playing with people. No point in having a fantastic game of golf if the game never shows itself in company. What is that about a great tree falling in the forest?

I had developed the routine of stopping in at the village shop on the way back from early golf to pick up the papers and milk. In this community a visit to the local shop played the same role as flicking on CNN in the States or checking your morning email. It's where you found out what was going on. Today the talk was of weed.

The weed had got a lot worse since it first appeared earlier in the summer. People were really steamed about it. Huge mounds of the stuff rotted along the high water mark of every beach. The first response of complete denial was no longer working. The theory had evolved that an unusual weather pattern was causing the weed. The warm summer had helped the weed flourish. I didn't dare say anything but the summer hadn't seemed unusually warm and the weed had been on these beaches for several years and was getting worse each year. Another deep thinker was of the view that we shouldn't call it the weed anymore, as this made it sound environmental and OK. We should just plain call it pollution.

27
A Dangerous Pause

*F*or the next six days I played no golf. Things were going extremely well in my quest for single figure play. They had never gone better. Looking back, it seems insane after so much work and now success, to lose six days. Of course, I didn't mean to lose these days. They crept up on me one day at a time. Days Forty-three and Forty-four I hit balls at the practice ground, but didn't roll out of bed in the morning for golf. On Day Forty-five the world of work interceded, one of those first flight of the day out, last flight back kind of days. No guilt there; golf was just not possible. Day Forty-six again brought no golf, as I felt I deserved a rest after a long day away the day before.

By Day Forty-Seven I was starting to feel really guilty about what had now grown to a four-day break in play. I set firm intentions to play nine holes in the evening. The trouble with planning the golf for later in the day is the day's events have a way of squeezing the golf out. Why is it that human nature always underestimates how long jobs take? The triumph of hope over experience that a complete day's work can get done by four p.m., allowing nine holes of evening golf.

People who get up crazily early to get their exercise in; jogging, lap swimming or whatever, had always seem nuts to me. Sometimes, early morning, as I perused the paper, sucking coffee to keep the eyes open, I'd see these types jogging down the road, exuding an air of irritating superiority. I often wondered if these people got up early and did all this just to make the rest of us feel bad. Now I could see the sense of the early morning thing. If you set your intentions to jog a certain number of times a week, or swim or golf, the way to ensure it gets done is get up and get it out of the way before the rest of the day starts.

On Day Forty-Eight, the alarm goes off at six. It's just getting light and rain is pouring down outside. No way any sensible golf could get done in this. The rain poured all day long as it only knows how to pour in Ireland.

One day at a time, I missed six days of golf. In my sixty-day push I had suddenly lost ten percent of my days, just when things were really starting to work. Why had this happened? Obviously, one can make excuses day by day for not going out. The reality is, if you really want to do something, you're out there doing it, not sitting back thinking up excuses.

Looking back, this stage was the second major challenge of my sixty-day program. The first challenge had come about two weeks in. At that stage I had worked hard but seen no progress. This second stage was different. There had been considerable improvement and reward. The challenge here was more mental fatigue. After forty days thinking about golf every day, it's very easy to get fed up with it.

The second issue was I'd seen vast improvement in my game. I was already scoring better than I ever had in my life. Maybe I was now good enough. What's wrong with just leaving things here? This is where the power of having a goal really helped. I'd set my intentions to do sixty days and try and get under ten and that is what I was going to do.

With a huge heave of will, I determined that however jaded I felt I would get up on each and every morning of the next twelve days, play nine holes and practice for an hour. I would push for that finishing tape.

Back at school I had always been consigned to the cross-country team, primarily because I was so rotten at the team ball sports. Cross-country meant running around large, muddy fields in an English winter. Strangely, I actually liked it. The last few hundred yards of the race were mentally the hardest. You were already exhausted but you had to give a final burst of speed to the finishing tape or risk losing your place to some hero whizzing past at the last minute. To make it more depressing, the general consensus among people who plan these things was that a good cross country course should always have an uphill finish. That feeling, at the end of a long race, of sprinting up a muddy English hill is pretty much summed up in Kipling's famous poem "If":

If you can force your heart and nerve and sinew
To serve your turn long after they are gone

When I first read that poem back at school I didn't much like the sound of those lines. I preferred more noble-sounding challenges, such as:

If you can talk with crowds and keep your virtue
Or walk with kings - nor lose the common touch

For me at present putting together a strong finish for my sixty days of golf was more akin to the final few hundred yards of a cross-country run, or that bit about nerves and sinews in Kipling.

Keeping my eye on the ten handicap goal was crucial at this stage. Years ago I was sent on a time management course. Just the sight of the overly enthusiastic man who was there to teach us all how to get a whole lot more done each day made me feel completely exhausted. He did say three things about goals that stuck in my mind:

- People with goals achieve more than people without goals.

- People who write their goals down are more likely to achieve their goals.

- People who look at their written goals periodically are more likely to achieve those goals.

Without doubt if I had not set myself the sixty day goal to get to a ten handicap I would not have pushed forward hard for the next two weeks.

Good intentions set for unbroken early morning golf I went up to the Pink for a drink, what else could you do, this was Ireland. The talk of the sale of the Pink had become huge. One wasn't supposed to talk about it in front of Bill so whispered comments when he wasn't looking. Rumour was that someone had heard that Bill had told someone, these someone's always remain a mystery in these stories, that he had the place sold.

Apparently Bill had said it was a local who was buying the Pink and we'd all be pleased. Of course there was intense interest in who that local might be. Like pebbles on a beach names were picked up, turned over, examined, discarded. We would all be very surprised when we found later that year who it really was who bought the Pink, stalking it silently all through the months of that summer. Mixed in with all this there is talk of a big developer. The Pink is to be knocked, they are going to build a huge hotel, someone had seen the plans. As I left that evening Bill called to me cheerily across the bar "the place will be sold by Friday."

Walking home after all the rain of the day, it was a beautiful still evening. The lights from across the bay reflected perfectly in the glass-calm sea. Electricity only came to these parts of rural Ireland in the mid 1950's. It sure must have been dark back when my father spent his childhood summers here. There's a blackness to the night here that is a shock to the city dweller. This blackness shows the stars in their full glory. A dense canopy of stars, vast numbers, more than can be seen around the lights of a city. Spend a brief time watching and you will see the mad dash of a shooting star, or a satellite making its stately progress across the sky. Seeing the rich fullness of the stars you can imagine ancient man's fascination with the heavens. For them their color TV.

At last I make it out to the course again for early morning golf. Just standing here on the first tee I feel that huge weight of guilt lift from my shoulders. After the six-day break, my play is rusty; I score forty-one with nineteen putts. The good news is hitting four greens. All that range practice with the irons is beginning to show. I'm hitting more greens and that is down to the irons.

28
The American Girlfriend and Castles

The talk back at the village shop that morning was of the American Girlfriend. She was causing huge interest. Everyone kept asking how things were going between them. Things had seemed frosty when she first arrived. The questions were constant: "How's it going?" "Are they getting along?" "Do you think she'll stay longer?" There was great hope in the village that things would go well between them.

The daily questions reached such a pitch that I suggested putting a swing-o-meter down at the boat slip, similar to the famous one used on television on British election nights to show the swing to Labour or Conservative. This swing-o-meter could be calibrated: frosty, warmer, friendly, very friendly, torrid. It had definitely started on frosty but was now reading "friendly," maybe even "very friendly."

The American Girlfriend had reached the stage of needing

things. The first issue had been ice, then email, then charging cables, then digital memory cards. All this would have been easy in a city, but in a small rural village each need was a challenge. There was tremendous determination in the community not to fail in any of these needs. Many surreptitious phone calls went from house to house, many furtive runs in the car down a country lane, to fill these needs with apparent casual ease.

To be fair, the first of these needs, ice, she never even asked for. She was coming for a drink and we were nervous not to have ice just in case she asked for it. Europeans harbour great fear of being caught short in the ice department by Americans.

There were a large number of refrigerators in different nooks and crannies of that big Georgian house. None of them had a fancy icemaker. Not one of them even had an ice tray.

We went to several local hardware stores searching for ice trays but always got the same comment: "There's not much call for ice around here." We had no ice and she'd be here in half an hour! I rushed to the Pink to fill a bucket of ice. When I got this ice back to the house it had semi-melted, then re-frozen itself into a giant iceberg. I had images of frantically hammering chunks off this berg.

On arriving, the American girlfriend requested white wine. No call for ice. After our ice escapades I felt moved to speak. I asked her if she needed a couple of ice cubes in her wine. She fixed me with a green gaze and said, "No, the wine is nicely chilled, thank you."

That evening the talk was of castles. It turned out what she really wanted to see was castles. There may be challenges in producing memory cards and computer cables around here, but castles are easy. History had left this land with layer upon layer of castles, some very old, some new.

The oldest castles were the Neolithic hill forts. The locals often call these the fairy forts, legend being they were built by the fairies. It is always odd hearing a big Irish farmer talking in a lilting Irish accent of the fairy forts on his land. They tell of unlikely tunnels linking one fairy fort to another. Much legend surrounding these forts is along the lines of "if you mess with them you'll die." Tales abound of old so-and-so down the valley, hale and hearty, who knocked a fairy fort and was dead within the year.

Each age of history left more layers of castles. Two thousand years ago the Celts built their famous round towers, tall needles, the doorways forty feet up. The builders welded the great stones together by setting huge fires at their base. The idea behind the towers was, if attacked, the defenders ran into the tower, pulled up the ladder and waited until the attackers got bored and went away. For entertainment they lobbed rocks out on the attackers' heads. Today many of these striking towers are incorporated into churches following the early Christian habit of co-opting pagan sites.

Eight centuries ago the Norman conquerors left great stone towers dotted across the land in an effort to control the crazy Celts. They found this was a hard thing to do. Today these massive, picturesque, ivy-clad ruins fall prey to the gentle brush of the watercolorist. It is strange to think that in their day the towers were high-tech military weapons, symbols of power, the B52s or cruise missiles of their time.

Churchill wrote, "Artillery spoke to Irish castles in a language they understood." His point was that older castles had high walls, thin but high. Hard to climb over and hard for a trebuchet to lob a rock over. With the advent of artillery, high was no longer good. Low, squat and thick was needed. The newer artillery-proof star forts lacked the scenic beauty of the older castles.

Then came the Victorians. Their castles were less about military might and more about economic might, splendid homes for the powerful and rich. The fashion was to add towers and turrets to the great houses to give them that castle look. Really these great structures were Victorian follies, not castles at all but Disneylands of their day.

When the American girlfriend asked for castles, it was a case of "so many castles, so little time." What sort of castles did she want to see? It turned out to be the great house with turret variety and, if possible, ivy-covered. This was easy.

29

Ten Days to Go and My Score's Getting Worse

Rain pushed play back to an afternoon round today. The course is crowded and I'm wedged firmly between a group in front that has me waiting on every tee and a group behind who lands balls on my heels. No time to mess about on the course today, a shock from the luxury of having the course completely to myself in the early morning.

I have exactly ten days to go to get my five game average score under ten, but for the past four games my score has gone inexorably up: 38, 40, 41 and today 42. I don't have much time left but my score is going steadily in the wrong direction.

Looking at the scores from those four rounds, the problem is not my fairway shots. I've taken exactly sixteen fairway shots on each of the four rounds. The difference in the score is the chipping and putting. Maybe it was the six-day break in play, but for some reason the short game is getting worse.

One aspect of the fairway game seemed noticeable. There were days when the woods worked well, the great feeling of good sweeping shots and there were days when the irons worked well. However, the woods and irons seldom, if ever, worked well on the same day. I was comforted by the comment from a friend who had been a sub-ten handicap for many years. He had always found the same thing himself. For him there were periods when the woods were great and periods when the irons were great, but greatness in both spheres never combined.

Rolling Average Number of Fairway Shots

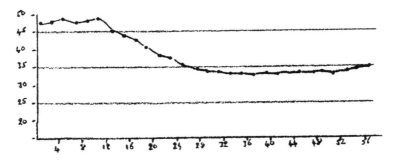

While standing back and philosophising about the process of improving a golf game, it seemed to me a big part of what goes on is a series of breakthroughs followed by disappointing let-downs. There are many days when you return home elated, walking on air, believing that you've really cracked some as-pect of the game. Next day the breakthrough has evaporated, leaving an intense feeling of disappointment and frustration.

After several weeks of riding this elation-frustration roller coaster, it becomes apparent that, while you never owned your breakthroughs forever, you also never fell back all the way. The process was a gradual ratchet, click by click improving your game. Once I realised this I found the process less frustrating. Fair enough, I would enjoy that feeling of elation as I drove home after something had started to work, but I would be philosophical that it would not necessarily be working the next day. Philosophy brought me a great bargain; I would enjoy the upswing of the roller coaster ride but lose the downswing.

This same philosophical bargain helped in the juxtaposition of performance on the range and performance on the course. Earlier in my golf quest I'd been given that little treasure of knowledge; hit a hundred seven-irons on the range. Next day, a seven-iron, hit under pressure on the course, will equal the worst of the hundred shots hit on the range. This realisation was a huge help to me. There had been vast frustration that on the range one could hit a whole bucket of seven-irons beautifully, but when out on the course trying to make a score next day the seven would be awful.

Years ago a Japanese friend gave me a great tip. Work on the range was like a long-term investment. The return did not come next day, but would be apparent in your game later. They are a philosophical lot, the Japanese. I came almost to fully expect that whatever I had worked with on the range the day before would be a disappointment on the course the next day, but that a week later the investment would show its colors. This thought helped me a lot. First, it helped me to be calmer and even find it funny, when some great triumph on the range refused to show its face on the course. Second, I found it to be true that work invested on the range did eventually show up on the course.

On the way home that day the gossip at the shop was about wedding invites. It turned out that for the big wedding of the summer some people would have to be left off the invite list. The cause of the crisis was a small church and a limit on the number of people who could fit in the reception marquee. This new crisis opened the door to enormous speculation about who might be left off the list. It was not so much about missing a great party, but the social ignominy of being excluded. There was a great deal of counting on fingers of people who absolutely had to be there. This highlighted how very few other invites there could be. What would life be without the daily gossip at the shop?

Driving home across the causeway I stopped the car and got out to enjoy the beauty of this scene. The Piano Player walked along the road coming fast from the other direction and passed without saying hello. I wondered why he never spoke but I suppose he speaks through his music.

I had driven across this causeway many hundreds of times but never grew tired of the beauty of this place. Sometimes the old causeway sat dry amid the golden sand, armies of sea birds taking their low-tide opportunity to feed furiously out on the flats. Sometimes the rich blue high-tide water rippled at the very top of the causeway.

Though today it is a scene of great beauty, the causeway was built in a time of immense suffering. It's what is known as a famine work. Built during the great potato famine, it was a public works project to create employment for the starving people. The Victorian morality of the time deemed it wrong to just hand out food to starving people; they should work to earn it. Thousands of construction projects were set up all over Ireland to create work; roads, bridges, causeways. My imagination conjured thoughts of people thin, weary and weak, literally dying of hunger, walking here every morning to carry these heavy stones and heave them one upon the other.

Coastal regions of Ireland are a lattice-work of old causeways and sea walls. The majority of these structures are not famine works. They were built during the pre-famine days of population explosion. The potato, discovered in "the New World" and brought back to Ireland, was an extraordinarily abundant crop in the Irish climate. A family of six to eight could live off the potato crop grown on just an acre and a half of land. This abundance of food triggered a huge explosion in the Irish population from 1770 to 1845.

No one can be sure what peak the pre-famine population reached. The census said just over eight million but it's thought there were really over nine million. The Irish population today, a hundred and sixty years later, is five and a half million. The pre-famine press of people put huge pressure on land. Land was gold. Fields were chipped out higher and higher up the hills and pushed out into the sea by means of sea walls, the enclosed land back-filled with sand and seaweed.

30
Chipping to the Box

I finally get some serious chipping practice going back at the house. It's a downsized version of Nathan's pitching at the buckets and the game comes about by accident.

I've been fiddling around with a few balls and an eight-iron out on the lawn, not really proper practice, more a way of avoiding doing something else. Displacement activity. To clear up the balls I distractedly chip them back to a cardboard box my son has left on the lawn. I think he mentioned this box is actually the Titanic. A couple of my shots bonk off the box, then one plops in with a pleasing thump. Becoming more focused, I try to put another ball in the box. I bonk one or two more off the side, but no more go in.

For some reason this game takes hold of my mind. How long would it take me to put all the balls into that box? I have fifty balls out on the lawn, one lone ball now in the box. Leaving that lone ball in the box, I collect the other forty-nine and chip them all again. This round not a single ball goes in. This is going to take a long time.

The first thing I figure is: if the ball isn't on the right line for the box it isn't going in. Rather than worry too much about the length of the chip shot I concentrate completely on the line. Relatively quickly I'm sending those chips out on a good line. The balls may not be going in but they lay in a pleasing cluster, short and long but in line with the box.

Once the line is working I start thinking more about the length. It seems to me I'm short more than long, so I correct by consciously trying to overshoot. It's kind of like ranging a naval gun. Working away with the same club, at the same distance, to the same target, I start to think of a phrase I had heard but not understood: feel and touch. These words are a bit like faith; you have to experience them before really knowing their meaning.

I spend several days working away, trying to get those fifty balls into that cardboard box. Little by little the rate of thumping in the box speeds up. At the end, the balls go in fast, sometimes three or four in a row. The endgame is a lone ball that refuses to go in. I chip it up, miss, go pick it up, walk back, over and over again. At last that damn ball goes in and the game is over.

I don't know how many hours I spent playing the box game – possibly four to five hours over three days – but it radically changed my chipping. I felt I finally understood. I had got it.

31
Working Hard at the Range

*E*very day I hit balls on the range. While in the early stages it was a real effort to get out and hit balls, by now it has become an easy habit. It has also become quick. Like other forms of activity, be it jogging, lap swimming or whatever, if you do it frequently you become very efficient at getting the bits and pieces you need to go do it. The transition time speeds up. At first, going to the range had been an hour and a half out of the day, but now it was a fast thirty to forty minutes.

Partly I was quicker because I was hitting fewer balls, more like forty to fifty balls in a session hit slowly and carefully rather than the ninety or more that I would do at the outset. I'd learned the lesson that doing too much in a session at the range was counterproductive.

I had also become careful which clubs I worked with at the range. When I had first taken up golf I'd been told to always work down through the bag when practising. Start with the wedge and go down through the clubs in twos,

finishing with the driver. This may be the exact opposite
of how you play a golf hole, but practising this way allows
the body to warm up.

By the time I got back from the States I had developed
the habit of lining up the wedge, nine, seven and five to
practice. Laying the clubs out at the start of hitting seemed
to help set my intentions of what I was going to do. I had
a habit at that stage of getting stuck on a particular club,
for example the nine and spending the complete practice
just working that club. Sometimes, when in a particularly
orderly mood, I'd actually put a little pile of ten balls in
front of each club.

My big problem at that stage was that I could hit the wedge
and the nine very nicely, maybe not very far, but good and
straight. But as I got to the seven, my nemesis, the fade
started to show. By the five and the longer irons the fade
was there in its full glory, thirty yards right bleeding all
the distance off the shot. The issue I was really trying to
crack on the range was getting rid of the fade on these
longer irons. It didn't really make sense to leave my real
problem clubs to the end of the practice when I was more
likely to be tired. Gradually I adjusted my club line-up,
first dropping the wedge to leave the nine, seven and five.
Later, just working on the seven and five focused my complete practice on my problem.

It seemed to me that the more I worked on the irons the
shorter they got. I couldn't figure this out. I suppose the

more I thought about the swing the more self-conscious and tight I became. I didn't like being so short with the irons but a low-handicap friend told me it's okay to be short if the distance is predictable – much better than hitting long and wild. The table below shows my club distances at this stage and compares them with those of a low-handicap friend.

Club Yardages

	Mine	Low Handicap
Wedge	80	100
Nine	100	125
Seven	125	135
Five	145	155

Julias Caesar's The Gallic Wars, which is basically a book about how to beat up the French, opens with the famous sentence, "Gaul may be divided into three parts." In similar fashion I found my range practices could be divided into two parts. For the first part, there were practices during which I felt calm, collected, controlled. For the second part, there were practices when I felt rushed, frustrated, annoyed. Unfortunately, more of my range practices tended to be of the second type. Those wonderful, fulfilling, calm practices were elusive rarities.

By planning my practice club by club, including how many balls I would hit with each club and generally hitting fewer balls, I found the calm, productive practice happened more often – not always, but more often. In addition I found that by consciously taking my time, especially a break between each club, helped. I developed the habit of sitting back on the wooden railing for a while between each club, looking at the scenery, watching the other golfers.

A huge part of the frustration in hitting balls is that you know what it should look like, but you just can't do it. A thought expressed to me years ago became comforting and even encouraging. My Japanese philosopher friend had told me that the golf swing is like a puzzle that each individual golfer has to solve. Each of our minds and bodies are different, so golf has handed all of us our own unique puzzle. This strange thought helped. Rather than being lost in annoyed frustration, I began to think of it as an intriguing challenge. I adopted the confident mentality that I would, one day, solve this puzzle. It was just a matter of time.

Swing thoughts are the big thing when hitting balls. Nicklaus said he could hold up to seven swing thoughts in his head when hitting but he felt that amateurs could hold only two or three. I honestly feel that for me there is room for only one swing thought in my head during the one second of my golf swing. That works for me. One swing thought at a time, out there on the range, I chase the swing puzzle around my body searching for the solution: lock the leg, turn the hip, swing slow, relax, keep it tight, right wrist.

Did I find the solution? Not entirely, but I did improve. Practice is a strange word. You practice the piano, you practice yoga, you practice golf. For all of these, practice means the same thing: going back again and again to work on something very difficult. You get a distinct feeling of banging your head against a wall, making no progress. But if you have the discipline to keep going back and bang your head on that wall, you do improve.

Do you achieve your dream? No, because your dream runs before you. My dream, just fifty days ago, was to be able to get the ball off the tee into the fairway. I could now do that easily and in grand form. So the dream moved on. Now it was to hit a crisp, straight five-iron and maybe, one day, do the same with the three.

32
Ghosts

*T*hat evening a bunch of teenagers were chatting in the kitchen of the Georgian house, they were telling us the house was haunted. I remembered again that this was the house in which my father vowed never to spend the night.

A doctor living a little down the hill always insisted he regularly heard the banshee in this valley. In Irish myth, the banshee is an attendant who follows the old families and none but them and wails upon their death. I asked the doctor how he knew it was the banshee and not something else. He replied darkly, "if you heard, you would know." His family nodded agreement; it seemed they too had heard the banshee.

Across the field the Ambassador lived in another ancient pile. I'm not sure how big an old house has to be to be a pile, but his house was definitely a pile. He was a retired British ambassador who came to live in southern Ireland at the height of the IRA troubles several decades earlier. On being asked if he thought this was dangerous, he replied that God protects both drunks and fools, so he should be covered on both counts. One evening at dinner, as he carved the roast beef, a bullet smashed through his dining room window, embedding itself in the wall behind his head. He told the police sergeant not to bother too much about this; he thought it was just one of the local lads having a bit of fun.

The Ambassador was a big proponent of dowsing, the ancient art of using two sticks to locate water. He had taken dowsing to a higher plane, using the technique to search for minerals, sunken treasure, even nuclear submarines and to assess the sausages in his fridge. While not a poor man, he had that reticence of throwing the smallest scrap of food away that all who went through British rationing in the Second World War could never shake off.

Rumour had it that his fridge was a biology experiment of half-mouldy food. He would cheerily open the fridge, pluck out a plate of sausages green with mould, dowse them to assess their health and, if they passed, eat them. It didn't kill him. He's now well up in his nineties, hale and hearty, dowsing his way through the world. Who knows if this kind of grand eccentricity gave Britain its empire, or lost it?

The Ambassador's big old house, with an ancient graveyard right beside, must be a major candidate for ghosts. On going away for a few days he would leave a large reel-to-reel tape recorder to document the silence of that big house. Listening to the tapes on his return, he would find the most extraordinary sounds of footsteps, doors closing and indistinct but human-like voices. One could say maybe these were just the sounds of other people coming into the house while he was away. Rather like the doctor down the hill who said if you heard the banshee "you would know," I listened to those tapes and I knew. The sounds sent a chill down my spine. The ghosts never worried the Ambassador; he felt they were friendly spirits there to watch over him.

There is nothing like a bunch of Irish teenagers telling ghost stories on a windy night, as a cloud of rooks swirl above the house, to raise goose bumps, not to mention a desire to turn on every light in the house and start searching the cupboards. They were all in agreement that the most haunted room was the bedroom with the big mahogany four-poster bed. It was in the oldest part of the house up by the bell tower.

They each told tales of sleeping in that room. All agreed that you never slept well there, all remembered weird and disturbing dreams. One spoke of waking to find a ghost draped over her face; not a phrase I'd heard before. I asked if she'd been scared. The fourteen-year-old replied confidently, "No, I'm not afraid of ghosts. I acknowledged the ghost's existence and commanded it to leave."

That same young lady spoke of a happier spirit. She had been walking down the long corridor I now use for putting and seen, in the great mirror at the end, her black and white dog which had died years before. She spun around to find the corridor empty. Her feeling here was that the dog's presence was a happy spirit come to tell her everything was all right.

It struck me that my two-year-old son was now sleeping in this most haunted room in the house. We'd put him at that end of the house as it was as far as possible from us. It appeared he slept better if we couldn't hear him. What was that thing about a tree falling in the forest, or a babe crying in the night, if nobody hears?

All this talk of ghosts and a few nights later I woke from a deep sleep with the distinct impression that I had heard someone putting golf balls in the long corridor outside our room. Switching a lot of lights on and peering nervously out, I looked down the corridor at the putter and golf balls and tried to remember if they were as I had left them. My imagination suggested the balls had moved. What depressed me was the ghost's putting seemed to be better than mine.

In the dark before dawn I sit waiting on the bench by the first tee. Setting out for the course at my usual time I arrived to find it too dark to start. That half-light that loses the ball mid-flight. The autumn mornings are closing in now. I sit in the still silence. I have never in my life been an early morning person. It seems a right strange turn of events to find myself out here waiting for it to get light.

I have the course completely to myself this morning. It's a wonderful opportunity for practice. There is a huge gulf between the golf I play on the practice ground and the golf I play on the course. Shots I can do with ease at the range I muff on the course. It has to be psychological. The way to beat this mental hang-up seems to be to do as much work on the course as possible, play rather than practice and play extra shots on the course.

These golden mornings when I have the entire course to myself are perfect opportunities to take my time and practice. Hitting two balls around isn't the way to do it. I have five spare balls in my pocket and plan to concentrate my time on the parts of the game that cause me trouble. There's no point in hitting five-drives when my driving is working. There is a great tendency to practice the areas that are good rather than work on the areas that are painful. I need to be constantly aware of this and consciously spend time on my weak areas.

I really work the approach shots, not so much the wedge and nine but the seven and five. There isn't much issue of leaving multiple pitch marks on the greens; with my longer irons I'm not hitting many greens at this stage. I'm also not taking big divots out of the fairways. This may be part of my problem: not hitting down properly.

One morning I come across a line of divots where someone has basically been using the fairway as a practice range. Those kind of deep, long, regular divots can only be made by a golfer who's a very good player. It's vandalism to treat the course that way. After seeing this damage I make a point of being overly careful with the course, always repairing more pitch marks than I make and seldom landing more than one ball on the green.

One issue with having a lot of balls out on the course is keeping a proper eye on the score ball. This is easily solved by using a different color for the score ball.

When I have those golden mornings alone on the course, I really put in some time chipping. Often I stop for ten minutes and just chip. This time spent chipping on real greens makes a huge difference to my short game.

I don't practice putting on the course; the putting green is fine for that. Anyway, to date I have spent far too little time putting altogether. If I miss a particularly stupid three-foot putt when playing I sometimes bang two or three in from the same distance to show myself that if I hit confidently, the short putts go in.

Time and again out on the course my first shot with the score ball is rotten. Quickly dropping another ball and taking a second swing with little or no thought, that second shot will often be perfect. A playing partner shared the quip, "there's a great golfer playing one shot behind me." Why is that second shot taken quickly and with little care, so often better than the first shot taken with infinite care? Maybe it's the lack of care that works. Those second shots are always more relaxed, the mind not getting in the way.

33
Slowing Down

*D*riving down the lane to the house after golf that day I met the American Girlfriend walking up the road. Even from a distance I knew something had changed. Looking a lot less dry-cleaned, she wore an old pair of jeans and a raggedy Irish sweater. Her whole demeanour was more relaxed. Obviously she was enjoying just walking up this lane, picking blackberries and looking at the birds. She had finally slowed down. Her yellow-highlighted guide book rush to see all the important things was gone, giving her the ability to finally see. So many people come here in such a rush to see everything, they end up not seeing Ireland at all.

It turned out that in this second week she had taken long walks across the big beach each morning. Slowing down, she had finally appreciated the beauty of where she was, rather than looking at the guide book to think where she should be.

As a kid I loved Star Trek. I remember one episode when

something odd caused Captain Kirk and Spock to speed up many hundreds of times faster than the rest of the crew. The result was the crew could no longer see Captain Kirk. They thought he had disappeared and Kirk could not communicate with his crew. Kirk whizzed about so fast the crew were just stationary lumps. I am often struck that visitors to Ireland can be like people trapped in this episode of Star Trek as they whiz about in their guide book-driven frenzy. The American Girlfriend had managed to slow down. She could now see Ireland and was happy.

Surprisingly, the same thing could happen to local people. A while ago I had been speaking to the farmer who worked the land in front of my father's house. He told me that for years he had wondered what on earth we were doing sitting in chairs out in front of the house looking at the sea. He said that when he was young the pressure of farm work and family, had kept him so busy he never felt he had time to look around. It was just in the last couple of years that he had suddenly become aware of the extraordinary beauty of the view that had been around him all his life.

Today, a ho-hum kind of round for a score of forty. It's one of those days when nothing is really working right, but it's heartening that even with everything a bit off I still shoot forty. I've learned that if I just keep struggling on, one shot at a time, I can succeed even if I'm not touched by brilliance.

I make one small change to what I'm doing that day. When I didn't get a par I start to write on my score card the main reason why par didn't happen. Right from the start, Nathan had me writing down three numbers for each hole: the score, the chips and the putts. Adding a comment column to my little note card proved a great addition.

The card for that day is shown below. The score that day was forty, with just two greens hit for the day. I chipped up and down on two holes, the first and the eighth. The seventeen putts is not bad. Two one-putts balance the three-putt to bring the putting below the magic figure of eighteen for nine holes.

Score Card – Day 52

1	3	1	1	
2	6	1	3	*really bad long putt*
3	6	1	2	*missed 3 ft putt*
4	5	1	2	
5	3	0	2	
6	5	1	2	
7	5	1	2	
8	3	1	1	
9	4	0	2	*missed 3 ft birdie putt*
Total	40	7	17	

The idea behind the comments is not to write an essay about each hole, but simply put in the main reason I didn't make par. For example, the par four second that day was a double bogey, with the added comment "really bad long putt." The first three figures meant I had taken two fairway shots, one chip, then three putts. In writing this book months later and remembering the second hole on that course, those three simple figures plus the comment allowed me to unravel what happened. A drive, a seven-iron approach shot probably falling short and right. A poor chip to the green leaving a lot of work to do. My comment then suggests an outstandingly bad long putt that still left me two putts to finish. It was a sloppy hole start to finish, but my comment highlights the worst mistake for the hole: that very bad long putt. That was where the double bogey came from.

In similar fashion the comment on the par five third hole shows a missed three-foot putt to give bogey. Again on the par four ninth the comment shows a missed three-foot birdie putt to give par. Looking at these comments at the end of the game the story was clear; my fairway game was not letting me down, but I had lost three strokes to very bad putting errors.

I did not write comments on all the bogey holes that day. The comments started that day as an afterthought but seemed so useful that in later rounds I made a point of putting a simple comment on every bogey hole to highlight the main error. If I could do this quest over again I'd put comments right from the start. I soon developed short-hand to simplify the comments. "Very bad long putt" became simply "LP." "Missed three-foot putt" became "3P." My cards had a lot of "2P's," "3P's," and "4P's" in those days. "BC" was bad chip; "7I" was a bad seven-iron.

On the way back I was surprised to see Bill out on the beach hitting golf balls. It was a real shock to see him doing anything but work at the Pink. I don't think I had ever before seen him not working. Early morning he'd be out moving beer crates or riding a mower rapidly backwards and forwards, cutting the huge lawns in front of the Pink. Cloaked by the sound of the mower you would see him in animated conversation with himself. All day long he was the face behind the bar. Late at night, as a lone drinker nursed his pint, Bill was still there behind the bar polishing a glass or sipping coffee.

Seeing Bill out on that beach reminded me of all the recent theories about the weed. The weather was no longer being blamed. Fingers were now pointed at the farmers. Over-fertilisation. Nitrate run-off. Algal blooms. Eutrification. Talk had turned scientific. It had even got to the pitch that specific farmers in specific fields were being blamed for the entire problem. If it was over-fertilisation causing this weed, it wasn't a lone farmer down by the water's edge, but everyone farming the thousands of fields in the two river basins whose water ends up in the bay.

How Am I Doing – Day 52

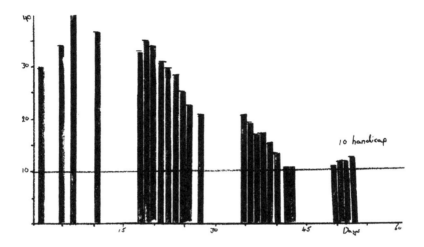

The graph of my handicap, based on the five score rolling average, shows just prior to day forty-five it was looking like I was making a direct run on the ten handicap line. My average handicap had fallen to 11.2. Following the six-day break in play my score started to creep back up and by day fifty-two my handicap was back up to 12.8.

My play is very strong this morning, the best I've known. I hit five greens in the nine holes, the most greens I have ever hit. My mind goes back to my early rounds of golf when I only hit two greens in the first eight rounds and had a run of six straight rounds when I didn't hit a single green. Things are certainly different now. The approach shots are starting to work. While it seems no progress was being made as I worked with my irons on the range, things are changing.

Partly I'm hitting greens by compensating for my fade, aiming way left of each green. It's hard to know if I'm getting the greens because I'm hitting better, or because I'm better at knowing how far each iron really goes and how far left to aim to compensate for the fade. The irons, even with their fades, must at least be consistent for me to be able to regularly compensate and get the green.

What's interesting is that with more greens hit, the pressure falls on the putting. Nineteen putts for this round is not so much about me putting badly, as more work goes to the putter. I hit five greens, but usually on the other side of the green from the pin. What's that phrase? "Up on stage but can't hear the band."

Driving back from golf each morning I had grown to look forward to what the buzz in the village shop might be that day. Today it was back to wedding invites. Tales of the splendour of this wedding grew day by day. Talk of the limited number of invites also grew. It was a perfect storm. The big talk that morning was that apparently someone had seen the list and had specific names of those who were not on the list. The thing was, nobody could say who this someone was; that was confidential. Also, nobody could agree on who was not being invited.

Average Greens Hit Per Nine Hole Round

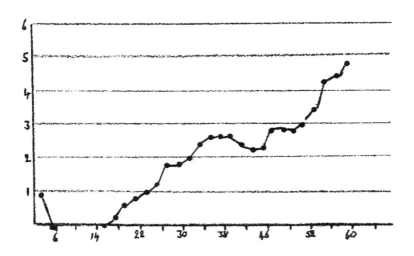

This graph shows the average number of greens hit per round. These numbers show a five round rolling average. The graph shows the first green hit on that first round, then the six-round gap before I found another green. Gradually the graph does show the inexorable rise in the number of greens being found, so that by day fifty-three I was averaging almost five greens hit per nine-hole round.

That evening there was a big night at the Pink and a send-off for the American Girlfriend, who was leaving next morning. A lot of people crowded in that small pub for a very late night. The swing-o-meter reporting on the relationship over the past couple of weeks would have shown the full swing, from "frosty" at first to "very good." The American Girlfriend had the ability to be introduced to a lot of people in a crowded room and remember all their names. I've always wished I could do that. Rather than pile all that calculus into our heads at school, which we never ever use, why not teach us how to remember a bunch of people's names?

Late, very late, the happy couple had a grand send-off through the front door and out into the night. We all wished them well and wondered what the future held for them. We had enjoyed the American Girlfriend being with us, like a film star in our midst.

As I slipped out of the Pink that night, it must have been two a.m., Bill muttered darkly from behind the bar that he'd still be washing the glasses here when he was eighty. I took this to mean that the sale of the Pink wasn't going well this week.

34
I Hit a Brick Wall

*J*ust six days left of the sixty-day quest to get to ten. I seem to have hit a brick wall. My five score rolling averaging swings back and forth between eleven and twelve, but goes no lower. Is this the best I can do? My golf is radically better than it has ever been, but maybe getting below ten is just not possible for me.

Days fifty-four and fifty-five brought scores of forty and thirty-nine, respectively, leaving the handicap average at 11.6, hovering tantalisingly above that target ten. That evening I phoned Nathan back in England for help. I gave a detailed explanation of the problem and was met with a pithy one-liner so typical of him: "Well, you'll just have to practice the putting." He had a cricket match to go to so that was the end of the conversation. Asking Nathan for advice and getting one-liners was a bit like those strange eastern films where the hero goes into the mountains to seek advice from the great Zen master only to receive a cryptic and indecipherable reply. The only difference here was that I was no hero and of all the human beings on the planet I could think of none less Zen-like than Nathan.

So much for Nathan's help, but his comment did get me to look at my golf scores from the past days. By now I had several days of scores annotated with comments. The answer was staring me in the face. Today's comments showed a three and a four-foot putt missed. Yesterday showed two similar short putts missed and a bad long putt. Everyday the same story: two, three and even four very simple putts missed. I only needed to save one of those putts each nine-hole round to sneak my game under ten.

My daily practice with the mid-irons on the range had become a pleasant habit. I was starting to make progress, I felt on the verge of solving the swing puzzle. The average number of greens I was hitting was clear evidence of this. At the beginning I really hated working on the range. Now I loved it, even looked forward to it. With a wrench of regret I realised I would have to move on, stop the range practice and give this time to the putting green. I set my mind to do no more on the range and spend an hour on the putting green every day from now until day sixty.

I felt really sad about this. After all my time with those irons I really felt I was on the verge of cracking them. Could I do both, the range and the putting? Not really. Partly I didn't have enough time; my whole day was not golf. I did have a day job. Partly I found that physically, but mostly mentally, there was only so much golf I could do. I just did not have the mental energy to work on the range and also put a good slug of time in on the putting green. I went to the range only one more time during the rest of the quest. My range days were over.

Day 55 – How Am I Doing

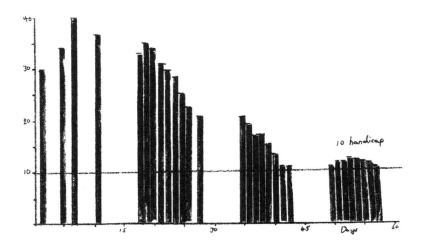

While the story told by my score over the past weeks shows me stuck, my game had radically transformed. A while ago these low scores – forty or just below –seemed just lucky. Today my play was strong, confident. I was getting these scores of thirty-nine and forty with ease. I had the feeling that there was plenty of gas in the tank to go lower.

At this stage of the quest I had become very aware that to be under ten I needed to average between four and five pars per nine-hole round. That's a score on this nine-hole loop averaging between thirty-eight and thirty-nine. By this stage I very seldom got double bogeys; similarly, I seldom got birdies.

35
Work Hard on the Putting Green

*T*hat very evening I go to the putting green. Armed with my putter and six balls I look at my watch and set my mind to spend exactly an hour on the practice green. My problem with putting practice in the past was boredom. I would set out to spend twenty minutes practising but after five minutes become utterly bored and walk away. For me, spending an hour practising putting is a big deal. I've never done it before in my life. That long hour reaches out before me and weighs heavy.

I begin with something Nicklaus suggested, placing a tee firmly in the green and putting to this tee. After you get used to aiming for a tee, when you switch to a golf hole it looks like a bucket. I find a straight uphill putt, press a long wooden tee in the ground and set about doing ten-foot putts towards that tee.

I start with this practice because I have no confidence in

my putting stroke. I'm conscious of my problem with the carpet putting; I frequently seem to push six inches right or pull six inches left. Ten feet out my putts can vary in line by a foot. It's certainly hard to sink a putt doing that. My other fear is that I haven't sorted out my alignment problem. Nathan proved to me that I was aiming right of the hole most of the time. I'm aware of this problem but not confident that it's been sorted. My typical miss is still short and right.

My thought is just to work away at a straight ten-foot putt to the tee until I'm consistently hitting it. Putting to a hole should be a piece of cake after that. At the start my results are terrible. I never hit the tee. I keep checking my watch. Five minutes down, fifty-five to go. Seven minutes down, fifty-three to go. Endless. I don't think I can stand an hour of this.

With great effort, I keep doing it. Gradually I look at my watch less. My results improve. I start to hit that tee a bit, then a bit more, then regularly. Soon I can plonk four balls in a row into the tee. This feels great. I furtively look around, hoping, maybe, someone sees how great I am. Nobody cares.

It got better than that. I notice sometimes the ball hits the tee and bounces back to the left, sometimes to the right. The direction of the bounce shows that while the ball hits the tee it's a bit left or right. Sometimes a ball hits the tee with a solid clunk, bouncing back straight. I've hit that tee dead on. Soon my game is not just about hitting the tee, by this time I'm hitting the tee almost every time, but about getting those dead-on hits. The reward for a dead-on hit is walking up and moving the ball, as it's sitting right in the line for the next putt.

Completely lost and happy in this seemingly mindless game, I suddenly realise that over an hour has gone by, flown by in fact. Rather than pack up and quit, I'm eager to try aiming at a hole rather than a tee.

Finding a ten foot uphill putt to a hole I confidently set about putting. After hitting the little thin tee, dropping balls consistently into the big bucket of a hole would be a easy. Missed all of them. Very frustrating. I thought if I moved up to four feet and put a few in from there I'd regain my confidence, then I could move back to eight or ten feet. Even from four feet most of my putts missed. Incredible. I could consistently hit a golf tee bang on from ten feet but couldn't sink the ball in the hole from four feet. This was the blatant power of the mind at work. The tee wasn't frightening but the hole brought up all sort of fears.

Driving home I felt greatly surprised that I had ended up spending an hour and twenty minutes on the putting green with no boredom. The time had flown by. Actually, it had been pleasant and peaceful. I felt elated about my work putting to the tee but annoyed that this success didn't translate to the hole.

There was a great story that day of Bill saving a dolphin

he'd found washed up on the beach in front of the Pink.
He had spent hours chest-high in freezing water holding
that dolphin so that it could keep breathing and finally be
coaxed back to open water. At one point Caroline, from up
at the Pink, drove by, climbed the wall and called down,
"I'll need to go fetch a bigger pan to cook that one, Bill!"
Bill glared up at her.

Next day, when the dolphin was found back on the beach
dead, Bill spent hours in floods of tears. Behind all his
fireworks, Bill had a real heart of gold. I glimpsed this a
couple of years earlier when my father was dying. Bill always asked after him. I could see in his eyes that he cared
deeply. He'd sometimes grab a bit of paper and pen a
beautiful note, there on the bar, writing quickly in elegant
handwriting that you don't often see these days. I'd take
those notes back to my Dad and read them. By then my
father couldn't speak anymore, but he'd smile when he
heard from his friend Bill. We kept those notes that Bill
wrote for my Dad.

For the rest of that week I spent an hour a day on the practice green and grew to enjoy the time. Each day I would
start just putting to that tee and this always seemed to
work. Next, some straight four-foot putts, then gradually
move back to six and even eight feet. Ten feet back was too
ambitious. Make it too hard and you knock your confidence rather than build it. I found the big thing was just to
sink a lot of putts, time and again hear that pleasing rattle
as the ball dropped and get used to the sound. The more

putts I dropped the fear of the hole receded. Rather than expecting to miss, I expected to sink putts.

As the week progressed my putting games moved on. I was astonished how different downhill putts were. It drove home how little I really knew about putting. Of course I knew the obvious, that they run faster downhill, but spending an hour alternating between straight six-foot uphill and straight six-foot downhill, one learns a lot. It struck me for the first time how much better it was, when chipping, to try and leave the ball below the hole rather than above. To date I just tried to get as near the pin as possible. It seemed an elegant nicety to be thinking of such things when chipping.

By the end of the week I finally started to work on breaking putts. I'd spent the entire week just doing straight uphill and downhill putts, I could easily have spent another month on the straight ones and still have a lot to learn.

Starting to work on the breaking putts, it really struck me how hard they were. There was no one answer: hit hard with little break or hit soft with big break. There were two completely different routes to the hole and an infinity of options in between. I knew it was just experience. The more one practiced the breaking putts the more it would work.

One practice did help me with the breaks. I knew there was a tendency to pick the line but not actually putt the chosen line. When putting, the subconscious would do a bit of correcting. I started picking out the line, then putting a golf ball on the chosen line up by the hole, say, one foot left. When putting, don't even think about the hole; just imagine you're trying to putt the ball to hit the other ball, rather like snooker. As if by magic, one sees the ball perform its elegant curl back to the hole. Out on the course one can't start laying golf balls down on a line, but one quickly gets used to picking out a leaf or other mark on the green and becoming completely absorbed in putting to this. I never did conquer the breaking putts. I'm still afraid of them. But this technique helped me.

36
Was that the
Zen of Putting

*L*ater in the week I had an extraordinary breakthrough with the straight uphill putts to the cup. I remembered my aunt's advice from years back: "just put a hundred putts in." One evening I set out to do one hundred straight up-hill putts from eight feet and carefully count how many go in. It took twenty-five minutes to do the hundred and an astonishing eighty-seven went in. As if by magic, my putts just couldn't miss, good strong putts straight up the hill and plonk in the cup every time.

I had that feeling of having it cracked that I'd experienced at other points in the quest. I clearly understood how to do it now, could never forget it. The feeling of elation was incredible. I decided I would repeat this "one-hundred putt" practice every day. I had images of once I had totally mastered straight up-hill putts, then doing the same with downhill, then breaks. It all seemed so clear to me. Next day, the same routine, but only thirty-five of one-hundred went in. Whatever I had understood the day before was now lost. For the next several days I tried the same thing and never got above forty-five sunk in a hundred.

I tried to think back and remember what I had been doing when I sank the eighty-seven putts. I remember that there was not a great deal of thought about the putt. I remember I wouldn't even look at the ball after I hit it; I'd keep my eyes on the spot where the ball had been and listen for the sound of it dropping. I remember complete confidence that each ball would go in. There are those stories of Japanese Zen archers who keep their eyes closed and let the arrow find the target itself. My putting that day had almost been like that. Was it the Zen of putting? Whatever I had that day, it seemed abundantly clear and simple while I was doing it, but I was never to recapture it.

37
Putting and Tai Chi

*A*fter several days of putting for an hour a day I was surprised to feel muscle-sore head to toe. Having played golf, walking fast and carrying my bag, for nearly two months, I was pretty fit at this stage. I was intrigued that an hour of putting could be any kind of exercise. I wondered if holding the body still and controlled for an hour was similar to Tai Ch'i. I'd never done Tai Ch'i. I'd enjoyed the adventure of seeing thousands upon thousands of people pack the wide and foggy early morning streets of Beijing as they performed the slow and beautiful Tai Ch'i evolutions. It's slow and controlled, but supposed to be great exercise. Maybe I was muscle-sore from the putting because I was just too tense.

I was out on the practice green at the same time each evening all week. At that time of day the bar in the clubhouse was busy with returning golfers. As they sat noisily over their post-game beers, they watched me out there, endlessly repeating the same four-foot putts and no doubt thought me some sort of nut. I probably did look like a nut, but I didn't care too much. What had happened to me? Sixty days ago I'd have been in there having a beer. No way I'd be out in the gathering gloom alone on the putting green. I mentioned this to a one-handicap friend of mine who remembered this same time in his game development. He said, "that's what it takes."

38
Thick Fog and Huge Hitters

Another thick autumn fog enveloped the course on day fifty-six and held on through that round despite the efforts of the sun to burn through. Walking to the sixth tee, I could just discern two figures already standing there. I had no idea anyone was ahead of me that morning. They invited me to join them. It was a father playing with his teenage son. They were both huge hitters. In that fog we had to walk down the fairway to discover how our drives had gone. Their balls were further down the sixth than I'd seen anyone hit, seventy yards past mine and I had hit well. While the rational part of me knew that long hitting was not where the score came from, the ego in me wished I could hit that far. That sword myth inside the driver has strong resonance.

The teenager was on the local school team. He was super keen and fun to watch. Like most players at that age he was more about hitting mighty shots than chipping and putting. As he played, like magic he dropped extra balls from his pocket and more shots flew. He had balls all over the course, energetically running between them. I thought

I was the only miscreant out here in the early morn playing multiple balls. It made me feel great to see someone
else doing the same.

On the 180-yard par three eighth, my playing companions
both hit powerful irons, each finding the green. With my
irons still being so short my only way to this green was the
three-wood. My shot didn't find the green but landed short
on the fringe. I was astonished how far some people hit their
irons. I think they had used fives or sixes to hit this green.

Down by the green I chipped to five feet from the pin,
then sank the putt for par. Neither of my big-hitting
partners made par. Chipping up and down, I scored better than the big hitters.

My time practising the putting showed up immediately in
the scores. It's a strange thing: while working on the putting
green one can really see the progress. When playing, one
can't see the progress; if anything, things seem worse as your
expectations are higher. It's when you add up the putts at the
end of the round that the pay-off is obvious. For the next two
rounds I had seventeen and sixteen putts, respectively. Before
starting the putting practice my putting had been more of the
order of eighteen and nineteen for nine holes.

Again that day my play felt scrappy, but the end result was a
score of thirty-nine. Often I seemed to struggle shot by shot
but end with a respectable score.

Talk these days at the village store was all about the weed. A fourth theory had emerged. First, we'd denied the weed existed, then blamed the weather and next the farmers. The farmers now blamed the houses. The new explanation was that all the new houses put pressure on water quality in the area. The economic boom of the past ten years had seen a great number of new houses; there were twice as many around here as fifteen years ago. People compared notes house by house around the bay, counting up the new ones. The talk was also of how many more bathrooms, toilets, washing machines and the like everyone had. Memories went back to when people only took a bath once a week before church.

Weed theories were now perfectly balanced between blaming the farmers and blaming the houses. Bill had a story that his black lab got stuck in the weed and passed out due to the fumes. With tears in his eyes he described carrying the poor dog in his arms up the hill. As he told the story, the dog sat growling beside him. Looked in fine health to me. You never can tell with Bill's stories. Others told of children being covered in rashes after playing in the weed. My mind turned to an image of my son sitting in a pile of it last week happily eating it.

But action was being taken, committees being formed. Weed committees to find the fact, pressure government, write letters to Dublin. Every local village had formed its own committee. Each local committee appointed members to sit on higher committees. The committee structures were Byzantine in complexity. More energy was now spent explaining and arguing about the committee structures than examining the weed problem. There was breath of scandal. It seemed one of the villages had sent two representatives to the higher committee when they were only allowed one.

Some had memories from childhood when weed was valuable rather than a menace. Back then, when storms brought weed to the beaches, farmers would come down with carts to collect the weed and spread it on their land; it was a natural fertiliser. People remembered scraping every last little bit of weed from the rocks. In Thomas O'Crowhan's poetic book The Islandman, the story of his childhood growing up on the Blasket Islands in the 1860s, he wrote of collecting weed at the low spring tides, spending hours up to his shoulders in the cold Atlantic sea, raking in weed. They were tough people living back then on those, now-deserted, wind-blasted rocks on Ireland's westernmost point. The low cost of modern nitrate fertilisers rendered the once valuable weed a useless menace to be left piled on the beach.

39
Finally Playing Eighteen Holes

To the golfer accustomed to always playing eighteen holes, it would seem incredible that the first time I actually played eighteen was on day fifty-eight of my quest. Nine holes had worked well for me. I would not have had time to play eighteen every day. In addition, settling for nine allowed me to slip out onto the course in quiet periods when I had the place to myself.

My original plan had been to play eighteen holes each day for the last week of my sixty days. I had even entertained thoughts of going out in style by finishing with five days of eighteen, then a final two days of thirty-six. Lack of time whittled these splendid dreams back to a couple of eighteen-hole rounds. The bigger plan would have been a great thing to do. There is nothing like just playing a lot of golf holes to quiet the mind and allow the golf to happen.

I had played the back nine of this course almost thirty

times but had never even seen the front. It was something of an adventure finally going off the first tee. I'd wondered what these holes were like. The round was respectable, forty-two on the front, thirty-six on the back, for a seventy-eight. This was the first time I had ever shot under eighty for eighteen holes. That thirty-six on the back nine holes that I now knew so well was my lowest score ever for that nine. Being warmed up by the time I reached those holes made them easier. I hit seven of the greens on that back nine, getting five pars plus a birdie.

The second day of eighteen holes, my forty-two on that unfamiliar front nine turned to a forty-seven. The difference was I had a couple of playing partners. My concentration and my confidence were still fragile things. The big problem when I played with others was a feeling of being rushed, especially on the short game. I had to get over this.

An added reason for my poor score on the front was I suddenly started hitting the irons straight. After weeks of striving to straighten those irons, it just happened. This was a good thing, a truly amazingly wonderful thing. The problem was I had become used to aiming way left of every green to compensate for the fade. If the iron suddenly went straight I was left way right. It was hard to handle my iron shots suddenly changing mid-round. The first time, one assumes it's a fluke. It took a few holes to figure it out and summon the courage to aim straight at the green.

My play on that front nine felt so disappointing that I very nearly quit when we turned to the back nine. There was a wait on the par three tenth. As I sat on the bench, feeling very upset over the forty-seven on the front, I was composing mumbled excuses in my head, ready to quit.

For some reason I stayed. I'm glad I did. My game on the back was utterly different. I shot a thirty-six on the back for the second day in a row. While the score was the same, the route was different. Yesterday I hit seven greens, today just three. While my approach shots were off, my short game was on, getting up and down on four holes for par. I had thirteen putts on the back – my best putting ever. Those hours on the putting green really showed.

Back in the bay there was huge excitement. The wedding invites had arrived. After all the talk and fear, it turned out everyone had been invited. It was going to be huge. Talk now turned to how on earth we would all fit in the church.

40
Did I Succeed

*D*ay sixty had finally arrived. That last day of my golf quest had me out for the usual early morning nine-hole round. These early morning nines that had been so very hard at first now seemed second nature.

There had been a big storm the night before. These autumn storms were harbingers of the changing season. The storm had left the greens thick with sticks and leaves. For each putt I had to clear a litter-free path from ball to hole.

As I cleared a path for each putt I was reminded of stories of the early sand green courses. On these courses, with greens composed of a sand-tar sludge, it was legal to scrape with a wooden board a perfectly flat corridor from ball to hole. Apparently, if you did the scraping right, you would never miss. In the early days of golf, before modern agronomy, grass types and irrigation made high-quality greens possible anywhere, sand greens were widespread. Today one hears tales that they are still to be found in places such as the Dakotas or Greenland. I've never seen one.

The nine holes that morning ended with five pars, four greens hit, one chip up and down and seventeen putts, for an overall score of thirty-eight. To be able to play golf like this would have been unimaginable to me sixty days ago when I played that first assessment round with Nathan.

Following that final nine on day sixty I went to the range to hit a small bucket of balls. I was intrigued about those irons that had suddenly become straight. On that back nine loop there was only call for me to hit four mid-irons, two fives and two sevens. With so few shots out on the course it's easy to think the straight shots may have been a fluke. I wanted to hit a bucket of balls and see what was going on. I hit some re-laxed, almost desultory, shots. The seven and five really were straight, with no fade. I hadn't been imagining things. After all my battling to straighten these clubs, they sorted themselves on the last couple of rounds. That final time on the range, I took a bucket of forty balls, hit half and walked away, leaving the pile of balls.

Driving back, I noticed that the storm last night had scoured the beaches completely clean of weed. The awful piles of rotting weed had vanished, revealing once more the wide expanses of golden beach. At the shop one of the locals pointed out that now the weed had gone nobody would do anymore about it until next summer when the weed appeared again. The big head of steam behind the weed committees would stop. She pointed out that the weed had been on the beaches every summer for seven years and was getting worse every year.

They say that the average soldiers on the ground in a great battle may not know for days or weeks that they were involved in a momentous occasion. For example, the troops at Waterloo would have been involved in many days of wild manoeuvre and skirmish before the big day that history now names Waterloo. Probably, for most of them, it would have been several days before they learned that day had been the decisive battle, the British had won and the battle had been named "Waterloo".

In similar fashion, it took a while to find out if I had reached my single figure goal. Driving home from my final round on day sixty I had no idea if my score of thirty-eight for the day was sufficient to slip my five-day average under ten. Back home I worked out the numbers and realised I had achieved my goal. My five day rolling average gave a 9.8 handicap. I stared at the computer screen. My feelings were a mixture of tremendous satisfaction mixed with an unexplainable sense of deflation. The quest that had filled my mind for sixty days was over.

How Did I Do – Day 60

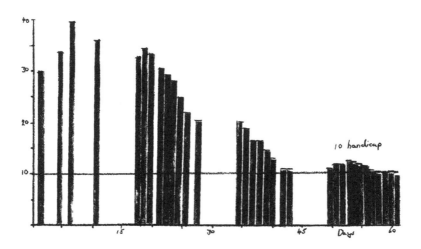

41
Leaving the Bay
I Love So Much

We were scheduled to leave the big Georgian House beside this beautiful bay the next day, so it was our last night at the Pink. To borrow the Irish expression, it was a grand night; a pack of people, the Piano Player banging out his music, pints of Guinness lined along the bar and far too late. As I walked out of the Pink, the Jolly Banker came out of the darkness and asked, "Do you know who bought the Pink?" I answered "no." But I did know. It was the Piano Player. He'd been the one all along, but he never breathed a word.

There is a rhythm to this place by the sea that goes beyond the daily rhythm of the birds, the monthly rhythm of the big tides, or the annual rhythm of the big storms. There is a rhythm to the talk, the talk that has always been so much a part of this land. With its glorious summers and long winters, there's an influx of people each year as the weather warms. Each spring, as the population swells, the pace of talk grows faster, the various stories unfolding through the season building to natural conclusions as the summer draws to a close. Through the long winter much of the talk grows silent, the stories rest, waiting to be picked up and moved on again next season.

I heard once a tape of the beautiful songs sung by the whales that gather around Hawaii each winter. These are haunting sounds that carry hundreds of miles through the ocean and can even be heard above the surface. The tones of these strange songs range from far below the reach of human hearing to far above. A single song sequence can last twenty minutes. These are the longest and most complex songs in the animal kingdom. What is truly fascinating is all the whales in the group sing the exact same long song in all its complexity. Careful listening to these songs has shown that through each season, in the waters around Hawaii, the song slowly and gradually evolves to become a different song. Then the song stops, the waters grow silent and the whales journey thousands of miles north, returning again to Hawaii the next year. On returning, the song starts once more. After months of silence, the whales pick up their song exactly where they left off. The song evolves once more in the coming season.

42
Setting Off to Play the Big Courses

*E*arly next morning as I left, the bay that I loved so much, conspired to be at its most beautiful, the sea glass-calm, the sky blue, a crystal sharpness to the air. I was setting off, with my family, on a four-day whistle-stop tour to take my newfound golf game to three of the famous big courses of Ireland. First would be the huge dunes at Ballybunion, then doubling back for the dramatic rocky peninsula at the Old Head of Kinsale and finally up to Dublin to play the exquisite links at Portmarnock. I was a little nervous how my golf game would stand up on these famous courses.

Driving cross-country through the fat of the land, first to Killarney, then on to Ballybunion, you get a good look at a big swathe of Ireland. At one point we stopped to look at a historic marker outside an ivy-covered stone archway. The plaque tells us this is a famine graveyard, later also used to bury the poor of the parish. Looking over the wall at this tiny strip of land, one sees a graveyard packed with countless stones. Not proper gravestones, just small shards of field rock stuck upright in the ground, some just a few inches high. Eeach small stone fragment marking a human life.

I knew how many people could be crammed in a tiny grave-yard. Mission Dolores in San Francisco has a graveyard no larger than a basketball court. Five thousand Miwoc Indi-ans lie buried in unmarked graves. A book, with chilling precision, records each death. Neat handwriting in straight columns lists the Christian name that the Spanish gave each Miwoc, the date they died and their age. This mission was the first building in San Francisco. The Spanish encouraged the Miwoc to come in from their villages and live around the Mission. The Indians died in huge numbers, succumb-ing to the new diseases brought by the Europeans. When the Spanish arrived, the San Francisco Bay had a population of around ten-thousand Miwocs. They had lived there for thousands of years. Within seventy-five years, the Miwocs were extinct, every last one dead. The last Miwoc left us this haunting quote:

"I am very old. When I was young my people were as plentiful as the grass. I had a son. I loved him. When the white men came he went away. I do not know where he is. I am the last of my people."

In Ireland, looking at this small famine graveyard, I won-dered at the thousands who may lie buried in this tiny strip of land. I wondered about the awfulness of their lives. The beauty of today's deep blue sky made the black history of the graveyard more terrible. Those jagged gravestones were broken teeth against the blue sky behind. The new prosperity had brought, almost to the gate of the grave-yard, a big road and a shop selling kitchen appliances. People now come to this place in shiny new cars buying their washing machines and cookers.

Further along the road, we passed a sign pointing down a country lane marking where Michael Collins had been assassinated. Following this small winding lane we came to a huge granite memorial at the roadside. This marked where Collins fell. Collins had been the central figure in the Irish fight against the British in the early twentieth century. His nickname was "the Big Fellow." He was a huge man. Of an evening, he enjoyed a friendly brawl with his associates. These so-called "friendlies" would often leave the pub where they were spending the eve-ning completely demolished.

Collins eventually participated in the peace treaty that gave Southern Ireland its independence but left the North with the British. At Ten Downing Street, as Collins signed the peace agreement, he looked up at Winston Churchill and said, "I'm signing my own death warrant here." He was right. There were those on the Irish side who were angry with Collins for allowing Ireland to be split. Those people did kill him. They gunned him down right here where we stood in a quiet country lane.

I had always imagined that Collins had been driving his car down a lane and was shot by a lone gunman hiding in the hedge. The write-up at the memorial told a different story of what must have been an big battle. Collins was actually travelling with several truckloads of troops and an armoured car. A large number of attackers ambushed this military column from the hills on both sides of the road. The ensuing fight raged for a mile up and down the lane, eventually leaving Collins dead in the road. It was strange to think of this violent turn of history happening in this peaceful place.

As we left, we passed a shop selling Michael Collins memorabilia, his picture plastered on cheap ("Made in China") plates, beer mugs, tea cups and the like. I wonder what the Big Fellow would have thought of that?

Having seen that large, grey granite cross marking where Collins died, as we drove on towards Killarney, I started to see many more grey granite crosses beside the road. These crosses, not as large as Collins's, marked where others had fallen. Each small cross, a death. Many crosses, reminders of a violent past.

We were going to stay the night at Glyn Castle before I played Ballybunion next day. Going through the huge front door of the castle, I had the feeling of entering Aladdin's cave. The walls and ceilings were dripping with antiques. This castle holds one of the most important collections of Irish antiques in private hands. The Knight of

Glyn, whose house this is, is said to be one of the country's leading experts on Irish antiques. On being shown to our room in this astonishing house, the family retainer, who moved sedately before us, told us this was actually the new house, built in 1720. He went on to inform us that the fourteenth Knight of Glyn was not currently in residence; he was giving a lecture to the Georgian Society of Dallas. My imagination conjured images of the Knight, in full armour, addressing the good ladies of Dallas.

Early next day I set off in a foggy, frosty morning along the Shannon estuary, towards the Ballybunion dunes. Breakfast in the great castle dining room had been fabulous: bacon, eggs, toast, marmalade, all the trimmings, happily munched in the great room of Glyn. As I ate, my two-year old son excitedly told me about dragons. The dragon carvings all over this old place had set his mind a-racing.

43
Ballybunion

*A*rriving at the Ballybunion course, there was a general air of mayhem. The frost had closed the course. This time of year the first tee is booked solid. Every ten minutes the frost delay continued, another four expensively-dressed men joined the crowd already hanging about. The course manager told me how unusual it was to have a frost right beside the sea and suggested I hit balls for a while. Following this advice, I took a small bucket to the range. I was hitting beautifully in that early morning frost. I felt the thrill of possibly posting a grand score on this famous course.

The only calm person in the growing panic, as the frost delay stretched out, was the starter. The fear in the crowd of expensively-dressed men was that the delay, if it went on too long, would mean they didn't get to play.

Watching the mayhem, I sipped a bucket of coffee the like of which I'd not seen since leaving the States. I pondered the old graveyard sitting right beside the first tee. That juxtaposition of joyful golf with death struck me as odd in my coffee-induced reverie. Those dead people lay there, day after day, as we the living happily hit golf balls over their heads. One particular grave, on the outside corner of the old graveyard, practically sat in the middle of the first fairway. I suppose there were golf nuts out there who would consider it an immense honour to be buried on the first fairway of this great cathedral of golf.

The sun eventually broke through and immediately the frost was gone. The starter went to work getting the crowd of expensively-dressed men off the tee. Watching him work I noticed how many of the players (mostly from the States) the starter knew by name. These wealthy guys must come here a lot and this starter must have a great memory.

Finally! It was my turn on the tee. I was hooked up with a couple of American players who turned out to be litigation lawyers from Washington, DC. They grandly told me how they made a point of coming to Ireland three or more times a year, just to play golf. That weekend they had been thinking of going to Pebble Beach, but from DC it was the same flight time to Ireland as to California. Changing their minds at the last minute, they came to Ireland. Nice for some.

My newfound lawyer friends teed off with beautiful shots down the first. I confidently teed off, only to completely fluff the shot. The caddy, who was carrying the lawyer's bags, looked shocked. Only decent players are supposed to be out on this course. I hadn't fluffed a tee shot like that for weeks. Why here, with everyone watching? Then again, the way golf works, especially here? Rather than risk fluffing a second shot with that crowd of expensively-dressed men watching, I opted not to score the hole. I hit a casual second shot from the fairway.

After that start I made an utter hash of the first four holes. The caddy and the two lawyers, were looking at me with an expression that very clearly said, "why on earth are you on this course?" The word "upset" would not begin to describe my feelings. A calming thought surfaced; "let's not worry about this first nine. Don't score any of it. Relax, enjoy the view and start scoring on the tenth." The instant I stopped trying to get a score, my game returned. The very next hole the caddy failed to suppress the surprise in his voice as he asked, "was that par?"

By the back nine, my game was truly grand. I was hitting the driver as beautifully as ever I had. On each tee, the caddie would show us the line. A line never had much meaning for me in the past as I really had no control on where my shot would go. Today I could thread a needle down that caddie's line. Every fairway my ball was up there level with the lawyers', sometimes in front. This was an utterly new experience for me, to be out on a top course with good players, keeping up.

The wind can be huge on these Irish links. It's particularly challenging at Ballybunion. The course switchbacks, one hole into the teeth of the wind, next hole with the wind behind. Time and again the caddy saved us from the wind.

On one tee we pulled out the drivers, only to see the caddie's dire shake of the head. "The six-iron is all you'll need here." The Big Lawyer, with wonderful panache, said, "I flew the Atlantic to hit my driver on this hole and I'm going to do it." The wind picked that drive up and the ball flew way beyond the fairway, dropping in deep rough. Chastened, we hit our little six-irons, the following wind performed its magic, carrying the shots far up the fairway.

The next hole was a 140-yard downhill par three with the wind in our face. The caddy announced that the driver was the club for this tee. Incredulously, we looked down the hole, imagining our drivers putting the ball way beyond the green into horrible trouble. The Big Lawyer was first up, his full driver into the teeth of that wind put his ball plumb in the middle of the green. I was next, a great drive, the wind picked up my ball, which seemed to go endlessly up, up and up into the clear blue sky, then dropped vertically, landing bang on the green about two feet from the Big Lawyer's ball.

This shot is burned in my memory as probably the most pleasing golf shot I have ever made.

Ballybunion is consistently ranked as one of the ten best courses in the world. To my eye the first few holes didn't seem much. Maybe there are subtleties to the design that my untutored eye can't see. One starts to wonder what all the fuss is about. Then the extraordinary genius of the course sets in. Golf course architects sometimes say eighteen holes of golf should have natural rhythm, like music, one hole to the next, the drama rising to a crescendo. Ballybunion does all this.

After the quite measured start of the first four holes the course builds in excitement, hole by hole. At the outset you are not aware of the dunes or the sea. After the flat early holes the course turns into the dunes and the sea is revealed. There is a feeling of "wow." This wow factor grows hole by hole until by the fifteenth you can't see how it could possibly get any better. But sixteen, then seventeen, then eighteen keep building, getting impossibly more outstanding. One walks off the eighteenth drunk with exhilaration. One is intrigued by the people who first looked at these great dunes and dared the dream of weaving a golf course through them. One is intrigued by the mind of the designer who planned this course, saving the best for last.

While for me the front nine at Ballybunion had been a blow-out, score-wise, on the back I took a respectable four over par.

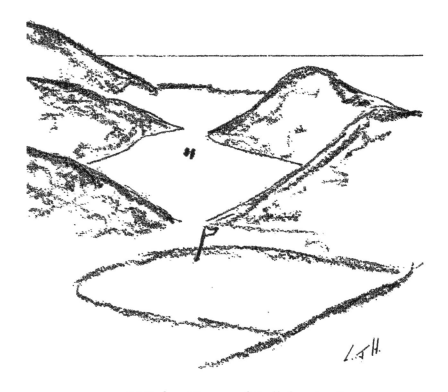

"Mighty Dunes of Ballybunion"

44
The Old Head of Kinsale

*A*fter Ballybunion, we back-tracked cross-country to play the Old Head of Kinsale. Ballybunion is old, founded in 1893. The Old Head is new, opening in 1997. This course must be one of the most dramatic views in golf. A rocky peninsula stretches out into the Atlantic, hundred-foot cliffs place the golfer way above the water. You look out over the vast circle of ocean.

It was off this rocky point at two p.m. on a Friday afternoon back in 1915 that a German submarine torpedoed and sank the great ocean liner Lusitania. The ship, almost as big as the Titanic, with 1,959 people on board, sank in eighteen minutes. The Titanic took two and a half hours to go down. Sinking that fast, there was huge loss of life; 1,198 people died, their bodies washed up on the beaches along this beautiful coast for days afterwards.

Over the years there has been a great deal of conspiracy theory about the sinking of the Lusitania. Some say that the Lusitania, though a civilian ship and not supposed to carry weapons, was loaded with explosives to feed the trenches of the First World War. Eye-witness accounts speak of a second, much larger explosion after the torpedo hit. Ballard, the underwater explorer who found the Titanic, recently dove on Lusitania. Titanic is two and a half miles down. Lusitania lies on its side in a few hundred feet of water; local fishermen regularly snag their nets on the wreck. It's relatively easy to explore Lusitania.

Ballard nailed the exact reason for the second big explosion. One of the torpedoes hit the Lusitania's massive coal bunker. This bunker, at the end of the ship's transatlantic run, was empty of coal, but full of coal dust. It was the coal dust, sparked by the torpedo, that exploded, ripping the ship apart from the inside.

It was a beautiful, sunny afternoon the day Lusitania sank. There were several groups who had come out from Cork to picnic on these spectacular cliffs where the golf course has now been built. These people would have been sitting, having their lunch, no doubt enthralled by the majestic view of the great liner coming fast over the horizon. The shock to this peaceful picnic scene as the massive ship blew up and immediately sank doesn't bear thinking about.

As a child I remember the last years of the great liners passing this coast before jet travel replaced them. My father would look up the shipping schedule in the paper and we would go up the hill behind the house to watch the huge ships cross the horizon, majestic and fast. When the ships passed at night, if the sea was still, you could hear the deep throb of their mighty engines coming through the water, even though the ship was miles out to sea.

Today, standing on the first tee of the Old Head golf course, no ocean liners had been seen in years. There were several fishing trawlers out there and directly below, the jaunty sight of the local lifeboat cavorting around the cliffs. Ahead on the course that day was a charity function in support of this lifeboat. The boat had come out to show off and it was a show. The hugely powerful engines sending the bright red boat in mad circles, its spectacular white wake painting letters across the ocean.

I was playing the Old Head with the Hurley Player. He was full of chatter, as he always is. A lot of talk about how well he was going to play and of course, how badly I was going to play. This chatter quickly stopped when I birdied the first hole. My game that day at Old Head was the reverse plan of Ballybunion. There, I started awful and ended good. Here I started good and ended not awful, but scrappy.

On some of the greens we almost had to fight big, black, crow-like birds with orange beaks and orange feet from moving the balls. There were hundreds of these birds picking insects from the greens. These were choughs, extremely rare birds on Europe's red data list. They were supposed to be rare but there were hundreds here. There's an odd fellow called the Bird Man of Baton Rouge who has discovered more new species of bird than any person alive. He is famous for saying that "every bird is common in its own place." The very rare chough was common at Old Head that day.

One of Old Head's greens hangs right on the cliff edge. Story has it that during construction a huge yellow earth-mover working on this green went over the edge, the driver jumping clear at the last moment. The machine's still down there, deep in the water.

The Old Head is long, 6,860 yards from the tees that we were playing that day. My driving was good; I was up in the fairway with the Hurley Player on each hole. My chips were great. One chip rolled right in. After all that time chipping balls into the cardboard box I often got lucky these days and had a chip roll in. My putting was a different story. Old Head's greens were much faster than anything I had played. I just couldn't figure them out. Bad putting that day left my score at ninety, the Hurley Player shot eighty-seven. He was back to chattering again.

Golfing performance aside, Old Head was a fabulous experience: a crystal clear autumn afternoon, the sea flat calm, massive views in every direction. We had to rush the last few holes as the autumn dusk was closing in. Our reward for being so late? An ocean sunset painted the vast sky with extraordinary colours. It was pitch black as we walked into the clubhouse for a pint of black Guinness.

45
Portmarnock

We drove north to Dublin to play the famous Portmarnock golf links. Dublin was a five-hour drive and those Irish roads are tiring. Ireland was halfway through upgrading its road network, so it was a patchwork of new and old. One moment we were cruising a four-lane highway, then presto, back to a winding two-lane road, stuck behind a hay truck. Some Irish drivers are obsessed with overtaking, they take no prisoners. Five hours of these roads feels like being trapped in a mad teenage video game.

Dublin is a big, vibrant city. Even at one a.m. the place is jumping, the streets crowded with people in party mood. It is also a very beautiful city. For a long time Dublin was the second city in the British Empire and probably the second largest city in the world after London. Wonderful Georgian architecture was built. During the 1960s and '70s, when much that was Georgian in London was destroyed by developers, the economic downturn in Ireland protected the Dublin Georgians. Today Dublin is a wealthy city, graced by beautiful Georgian streets and squares.

Strolling through one of these squares, I noticed a historic marker on one of the fine buildings and was surprised to read that this house was the birthplace of the Duke of Wellington. The Iron Duke, the great victor of Waterloo, who has gone down in history as one of England's greatest heroes. But here he was, born in Ireland! Thinking about it, rather a lot of "British" heroes turn out to be Irish; T.E. Lawrence, better known as Lawrence of Arabia, General Montgomery, Shackleton of South Pole fame, all Irish.

Early next morning I headed out of the city for a seven thirty a.m. tee time at Portmarnock. Leaving the city was easy, but coming in looked like a nightmare. Even that early all the roads in were solid traffic jams.

The Portmarnock course was started back in 1894. Originally it was a five-hundred acre sandy island, the founders rowed out to view the site in a small boat. Later, golf members were brought out to the island through the shallow seawater in high, horse-drawn carriages. Today a road took me through flat, marshy land.

The course was all but deserted. The pro, alone in his big shop and two ancient golfers going off the first tee. This was the biggest tee I had ever seen, the size of two grass tennis courts placed end to end. The clubhouse was in the midst of a major renovation. I was struck by the massive piles of white insulation stacked outside, ready to go into the building. It must get really cold here as the wind races off the Irish Sea.

I had hoped to play the course with my cousin the Jolly Banker, who was a member here, but he'd gone off to Australia to watch a Rugby match. So here I was playing alone, following those two ancient members. Watching those two ancient fellows methodically tee off and stroll slowly down the fairway, I was worried they might hold me up.

I had a nice drive on the first, my approach shot found the green and a two-putt for par. A steady beginning very different from the chaos of my start at Ballybunion. Big rain was forecast, I hoped to get as much of the eighteen in before it rained, I fully expected to get soaked.

There was something magical about those two ancient golfers ahead of me. They never seemed to move, or if any motion could be detected it was very slow. They teed up slowly, walked slowly, appeared to spend an age on the green motionless, poised like herons stalking a fish. The odd thing was, however fast I played, the ancient golfers drew steadily ahead of me, eventually to disappear. I watched them but had no idea how they did this.

My fear of being held up was replaced by a fear of getting lost. The course had no course furniture, certainly no big signs saying "this way to the next tee." With the disappearance of the ancient golfers I had nobody to follow.

Walking off each green I was faced with an IQ test. Little paths led off through the dunes in all directions. Which one to the next tee? On one tee I could not for the life of me work out which direction to go. Many of the tees have a long carry over dunes to find the fairway. This tee was surrounded by dunes and I couldn't see a fairway anywhere. Walking to the top of the biggest dune, I looked around for the next hole. I was horrified to see an endless sea of dunes in all directions. I couldn't even see the clubhouse. I felt lost amidst a mighty ocean, the waves frozen as dunes.

The long carries off Portmarnock were interesting. Often all one had to rely on was a white stone showing the line. Hitting the drive out on this line, the ball soars away, appearing to be lost amidst the dunes. Following a little grass path weaving between these dunes, one discovers a rich fairway, my ball sitting neatly in the middle.

From the white tees that day, the course played 6,900 yards, longer than I was used to. I was hitting great drives, but time and again was left with a 160 to 170 yard approach shot on the par fours. These long-iron approach shots were still the big hole in my game. A bit shorter and my irons were good, a bit longer and my three-wood was good. Compounding the length problem, the wind had gradually got up following the early morning stillness.

The par three fifteenth by the ocean is sometimes thought of as the signature hole at Portmarnock. On the tee I chatted with one of the greens staff who recounted watching Tiger play this hole the previous summer. Tiger hit the most extraordinary shot forty five degrees out to sea. As the ball soared out over the ocean a watery splash seemed the only possible conclusion. The wind picked that ball up and blew it straight back to land two feet from the pin. The green keeper marvelled that anyone could judge the wind that accurately.

I finished with an eighty-five that day and was happy. This was a long course with well-defended fast greens, probably the hardest course I had played to date. I knew if I had a second run at the course I could shave shots. Though I was alone out here and my head was addled from the constant buffeting of the wind, as I took my last putt I felt this was something of a momentous occasion. I had set out to work on my golf game for sixty days, then take my new game to three of the big-name Irish courses. That little three-foot putt at Portmarnock completed my quest. I felt a tremendous surge of accomplishment as I picked that ball from the hole. I felt like throwing the ball in victory to the invisible crowd on this deserted course.

As I walked from the eighteenth green, the rain that had threatened all morning came down. The Irish would say, "I felt a terrible thirst." The temporary structure standing in for the part-renovated clubhouse was uninviting. I drove back into Dublin and found a pub with a big open fire.

My quest began with finding a little pub in Kinsale where Nathan gave me the good news and the bad news. My quest finished with finding a little pub in central Dublin were I sat by a fire, munched a toasted sandwich, drank a pint of Guinness and felt tremendously satisfied. As I finished that sandwich a great tiredness came over me. I lay sideways on the pub bench and fell fast asleep. I slept warmly all afternoon amidst the noise of the pub. I don't know if this tiredness came from the morning's early start, the fresh wind of the Portmarnock links, or the satisfaction of completing my quest.

46
After it was Finished

After my golf quest, I was literally walking around in a state of amazement. I had achieved something that had seemed impossible and it was an incredible feeling. I had never in my life been good at a sport.

Though I started my quest not enjoying golf, I now love to play. Even better, I can go out with good players and really keep up, send my ball way up the fairway with theirs and battle the score out hole by hole.

The course is no longer the enemy. When golf is a struggle, I yearned for a wide, straight, open interstate freeway of a golf course. No hazards. No funny business to bother me. My new game allows me to see and appreciate the more interesting courses. Now that I have gained control of where my ball will go, the strategy and mental game of playing great courses is enthralling.

There is a powerful, energising feeling in pursuing a quest. A powerful sense of purpose. Strangely, though I averaged

about four and a half hours a day working on my game, I am certain this quest gave me time, it didn't take time. With a strong sense of purpose, one stops wasting time. Everything gets done a lot faster, one gains energy to do more.
An unexpected side effect was losing a nice bit of weight. That wonderful feeling of the belt being a couple of notches in and the trouser waistline feeling loose. I hadn't really noticed as this happened but I suppose getting up each morning and walking a fast nine carrying a bag, some good exercise there.

Was I a single figure player? No. Probably not. Certainly on the nine-hole loop that I had played over and over I was averaging single figure play. This course was no cakewalk. The eighteen was a 6,600 yard par seventy-one with a slope of 127. I didn't put cards in at this course as I finished my quest. I wish I had clocked a proper handicap as I crossed the sixty-day finishing tape.

I still had an un-set pudding of a game. When I took my game out and about, I lacked the experience to put in single figure scores. On unfamiliar courses, my scores were in the low to mid-eighties. There was still a lot of work to do to polish and bed down my new-won game.

Certainly I felt there was gas in the tank for further improvement. My mid-irons had only straightened up in the last few rounds. Absolutely this led to me to hitting more greens, but I was still coming to terms with this newfound straightness. The siren promise of the higher fairway woods, the five, seven and maybe even the nine, were worth exploring to address the continuing woes of my long irons. Definitely more room for growth in my putting, it was just in the last ten days that I had started doing focused putting practice. Yes, I could see clear areas for more improvement, with no feeling of having hit the wall.

Stupidly, I didn't hit another ball for four months after I walking off that eighteenth green at Portmanoch. It was back to the States for me and life got busy. The next time I played golf I was in Florida and the majesty of my new game had all but deserted me. It was a shock.

With a few days work I re-won my plush new game. It was still in there, just rusty. More important was the knowledge of how to practice. Even more important was the confidence that I could play golf well. I really could do it.

47

An Expanded Sense of Possibility

*D*own in the trenches, day by day, for the sixty days of golf, it had seemed like hard going. When I finished, had a great golf game and felt euphoric about the whole thing, looking back it wasn't that hard. Two months, four and a half hours a day, finished each morning by ten thirty. I'd done this astonishing thing. Got my golf game from nowhere to under ten in two months. The impossible now seemed easy. I was filled with a powerful sense of possibility, what other things were possible.

Completing the golf quest changed me. Change entered many parts of my life. It is four years now since that wonderful two months in an Irish summer when I did my golf quest. The sense of possibility the quest gave me changed the course of my life. In small ways and big ways.

There are many hundreds of small changes, so many that change is really a theme. Just one example of a small change was learning to do a tumble turn in the pool. I had swum laps for twenty years and had always been impressed by those people who did the fast tumble turns at the end of each lane. I always wanted to do that. Armed with that new sense of possibility, I stopped wanting to do it and just started doing it. At first I didn't know what I was doing. Early attempts were a tumbled mess. A flurry of arms, legs, bubbles, confusion. I'd often come up in the wrong lane going in the wrong direction. I kept trying and soon, I could do that tumble turn.

I'd played the piano for fifteen years. I was stuck in a rut and didn't even know it. I thought I was moving forward, playing new material, growing. Really I kept picking the same kind of stuff. Following the quest my playing changed, I started playing completely different music, my technique expanded. I even started composing my own pieces. Never in my wildest imagination did I ever think I'd be doing that. I was so excited about this, it was almost intoxicating.

Even my work changed. I had done pretty much the same kind of work for twenty years. Fair enough my work had grown and expanded, but really it was more of the same stuff. Today I am still working in the same industry but in a completely different role. Really a new career. This change has been huge and truly wonderful.

Writing this book is change. I've never written a book before. Writing this book was a harder, more scary thing, than doing the golf. Really it's part of the same quest. Once you embark on a quest, the spirit of quest never ends. You reach one hilltop and see another before you and decide to go there, climb that one too, because now you know you can.

I met a man who fixed a car. I was at a dinner I didn't want to go to, sitting in a chair I didn't like, next to a man I didn't want to talk to. He started telling me about a vintage car he'd done up years ago. I really wasn't that interested.

Suddenly one innocent phrase in his story made me intensely interested "As I came over the hill and saw the car I thought – oh no." He was describing that first moment he saw the wreck of the car sitting in a field, weeds growing out of it. It was the exact model he'd always dreamed of renovating. That feeling of "oh no, now what excuse do I have not to follow my dream."

It was the feeling I had at the start of my golf quest, when Nathan put the thought of single figures in a summer in my head, he had August free, I had been lent the house in Ireland, I had the time available to do it. That feeling of inconvenience "why now, why not later, oh no – what excuse do I have not to do this."

I realized fixing that car had been this man's quest. He spent a year of his life renovating that car, day and night out in the workshop. Now I was full of questions. All the elements of a quest were right there in his story. That feeling of inconvenience and fear when he set out. The doubt, the feeling that he couldn't do it. He'd had a guide, a mentor who'd renovated a vintage car before. The crisis, when he'd taken the car completely apart, parts laid out all across the floor, the fear he could never put it together again. That great feeling when he'd finished and he took the car to shows, won awards. Most importantly, the change. He'd fixed this car twenty years ago. I asked how fixing this car had changed him. He thought about it and said "I did something I thought I could never do. I take more risks now, since then I've done a lot of things I would never have done before."

The man who fixed a car opened my eyes. I realized that quests are all around us. Each of us has our quest, our call. The quest comes in a different ways for each of us. Often unexpected. Often inconvenient.

I met a lady who nearly died. She'd had a brush with cancer. I didn't know her well during the dark days of her battle but I had seen her from afar. The chemo made her sick, her hair fell out, fear was in her eyes. Walking beside her one evening she told me that today was a special day. She'd just had her five year blood test and she was clear of cancer. Every month for five years she'd had the blood test to see if there was any sign of the cancer returning. The five year test is big, if you are clear for five years, you've made it.

We stood under a Texas twilight sky, deep blue so blue it's almost black. Still too light for the stars but shining brightly, alone in that blue black sky, a perfect crescent moon, the bright white dot of Venus beside. She stood beside me alive and happy, her whole life before her once more.

I asked her how her life was different today than in those days, five years and more ago, before her cancer. She said life was so much better, more interesting, more vibrant, she truly deeply appreciated every day.

I realized this battle with cancer had been her quest. Clearly she didn't choose this quest, it chose her. I realized nobody chooses their quest, the quest chooses you. The choice you have is whether to accept that call. This lady, standing alive and happy, happier than she had been before, did have a choice, she could have chosen not to fight.

It's easy to think that quests are about knights in shining armour riding to rescue maidens in the tallest tower, pilots battling in space around other worlds, heroes fighting dragons in their mountain lairs. It's easy to feel that quests are for other people, in other places, in other times. The hero's quest is a major element of mythology. There's that wonderful Joseph Campbell quote "Myth is what never was, but always is."

Myth has such strong resonance with us because it reaches to the very basic programming of who we are. The Hero's quest speaks to us so loudly from mythology as it is an important part of our life experience. We will all be offered our quest; our challenge is: do we have the courage to accept?

The quest will come in many forms, many guises but the basic components will always be there. The whisper of the universe calling you. The sense of annoyance and inconvenience. The feeling that you can't do it. There will be a guide or mentor who will set out with you but may well abandon you along the way. A point of crisis when you are sorely temped to quit. You will meet unexpected teachers along the way. You will finish the quest alone. The extraordinary feeling of accomplishment when you complete your quest. Afterwards you will be changed.

I watched a top spinning on a table. Left alone it spun upright, stationary and happy in the same place. Lightly touched by a finger the top now moves across that table never to be stationary again. Some may look at this and feel the top was better left alone spinning steadily in the same place. Some may look at this and feel the top's brief chance to spin is so much more interesting when it moves. The quest in our lives is the touch of that finger.

The quest leaves you forever changed. There is magic in this change for it also creates change in the world and the people, around you.

www.Singlefigurequest.com